Five Cards and a Cathouse

Ken Hodge

A Wings ePress, Inc.
Young Adult Memoir

Wings ePress, Inc.

Edited by: Jeanne Smith
Copy Edited by: Joan C. Powell
Executive Editor: Jeanne Smith
Cover Artist: Trisha FitzGerald-Jung
Boy Image by Pixabay

All rights reserved

Names, characters and incidents depicted in this book are products of the author's imagination or are used fictitiously. Any resemblance to actual events, locales, organizations, or persons, living or dead, is entirely coincidental and beyond the intent of the author or the publisher.

No part of this book may be reproduced or transmitted in any form or by any means, electronic or mechanical, including photocopying, recording, or by any information storage and retrieval system, without permission in writing from the publisher.

Wings ePress Books
www.wingsepress.com

Copyright © 2021 by: Ken Hodge
ISBN-13: 978-1-61309-542-3

Published In the United States Of America

Wings ePress Inc.
3000 N. Rock Road
Newton, KS 67114

Dedication

To Linda Bruce, whose counsel and computer skills were invaluable.

* * *

One

"Hamilton!"

Oh-oh, the old H-word. It's my name, sure, but I hate hearing it yelled out like that. Especially from Mom. It means she's getting herself all pissed off at me.

"Hamilton Skutt!"

Holy crap, the whole nine yards—now she's *really* pissed!

"Come on, we're ready to go!"

What's the big hurry? It's not like we gotta dodge some huge landslide or duck some crappy earthquake. It's not like I don't know when to get in the car on a move. Hell, we must've moved a million times since I was a little kid back in The Dalles.

"Will you hurry up? The van will get there first at this rate!"

"Okay, okay. I'm coming right now, okay?"

They're all waiting in the car—Mom, Dad, my older sister, Veronica, and my kid brother, Skipper. His real name is Randolph but we call him Skipper. My oldest sister, Evelyn, isn't around anymore.

She married some guy who got drafted and now she's chasing him to a bunch of little Army towns all over the country.

I climb in the back seat of our '39 Plymouth Road King, the car Dad bought before our trip down to the World's Fair in San Francisco. "Peace in the Pacific" was the theme. I told Skipper Japan should win the peace prize 'cause they had a big pagoda full of geisha girls spinning silk, for God's sake! Pearl Harbor! Just like a bunch of lousy grownups to pull a rotten trick like that. But it's not only the Japs. I don't trust grownups, period. Seems like they rig everything. Seems like they know all kinds of stuff they keep up their sleeves.

Like that time in Redmond, in the barbershop. They're all laughing about some politician getting a stroke in a cathouse. So how come nobody told me what a cathouse was? And that contest the drug store ran. For a brand-new Schwinn bicycle to the kid who sold the most bottles of that Elixir of Youth crud. I sold eight bottles—using my "trap line" of Dad's employees—and got eight coupons. I knew that was enough to win. I kept the coupons in a safe place, in a little dish up on the fireplace mantel where Skipper couldn't screw with 'em. I was waiting for the big payoff when Mom had a visit from the mother of that phony Bryan Nordquist. She told Mom her son had tried hard but hadn't sold a single bottle and would probably get an inferiority complex. Then, I swear to God, Mom handed over all eight coupons! Just like that—Poof!— and all my scheming and hard work down the drain! If your own mom is willing to give you the shaft, you better be on guard against all grownups, always!

Dad shoves the gearshift in reverse and backs out on the highway. We live on Highway 97 right there in Madras—the best little old cow town in central Oregon—and we're moving to Pendleton, the biggest and best cow town anywhere. I could've driven us there myself. I'm too young to get a driver's license, sure, but Dad taught me to drive last year. That's so I could chauffeur him out to some old ranch and pick him up at the end of a stupid field when he was done shooting pheasants. Some guys might say that was a pain-in-the-ass, but I didn't mind too much—it gave me a good chance to practice driving. He pulls a left and we crawl along the one-block main drag. It seems like only yesterday we moved into this tiny town of board sidewalks and false-front stores, looking like a Gene Autry movie set. Dad's an engineer with the state highways and gets transferred about every four years. So we moved from Redmond, where I was born, to The Dalles, back to Redmond, then to Madras, and now to Pendleton. We pass a sergeant parking an Army jeep in front of the grocery store. It's 1943 and the Second World War is going full blast. Little old Madras even has its own Air Corps B-17 bomber base up on Agency Plains, on the plateau above the rimrock.

We clear the main drag and head north on Highway 97. I'm looking forward to Pendleton, this big city of ten thousand. But in a way I hate leaving Madras. There's a girl—Beverly Nelson is her name—who's gorgeous. She's beautiful. She looks like Linda Darnell, my favorite movie star. She lives on a ranch along Trout Creek, so far out of town I couldn't even take her to a stupid movie. All I could do was flirt with her in school, for God's sake. Madras still has some old pioneer customs. Like the box social.

At one of those, I borrowed money from Mom to outbid that bastard Mark Collins for Beverly's entry. We took her picnic lunch, wrapped up like a birthday gift, over to a corner of the gym. We opened the box and silently ate the goodies she had fixed. Big deal, right? Not so fast. It *was* a big deal to me. It was like a real date and I got a big thrill out of it.

We follow Highway 97 north through a familiar desert of sagebrush and juniper trees. Quiet as hell, no sound except our own car. Hard to believe there's a war going on overseas. Only way we know about this war is the scrap-iron drives and rationing and draft boards grabbing guys just out of high school. Oh, and the Japanese-Americans going to concentration camps. The feds set up a "pick-up zone" from the coast to this very highway. Say you're Japanese-American. You live on the east side of Highway 97, you're okay. But live on the west side, you're a spy and get sent to a concentration camp. You and your whole family. I heard some talk once in the hardware store about this. A guy says, "If the Japs didn't wanna go to the camps, they shouldn't have bombed Pearl Harbor." Okay, that made sense, I guess. But I felt bad about it anyway.

We drop down into a broad green valley of grazing cattle. The war keeps coming up in my head. Can't believe they're fighting out in the Pacific and in places like North Africa. Guys not much older than me over there getting their asses shot off. I used to feel guilty about it, but not anymore. Was it my fault I was born a few years late for this? Hell's bells, I could grab a rifle and go running up a hill toward the enemy, just like in the movies, maybe take a couple rounds, and what the hell difference would it make? Even if I captured a couple hundred Germans, like Sergeant York, I know I wouldn't get to be a hero. I know I wouldn't come home to a ticker-tape parade and stay in the Waldorf-Astoria and get paid to endorse some jock-itch ointment. Sure as hell, some captain would take the credit and I'd be left standing out in the rain guarding all those bedraggled krauts I brought in from the war.

Dad cruises along the highway, past a little store called Willowdale, and over the Trout Creek bridge. I look over at the Nelson ranch home base, picture-perfect with its hip-roof barn and big gabled house among poplar trees. I think about how magic that place is to me, the house where Beverly Nelson lives. That's the trouble, though. She lives on this ranch way out of town. So I couldn't even buy her a Coke at the drug store. Only time I got anywhere with this romance was right after our eighth-grade graduation ceremony. Mom threw a party at our house. The parents sat around in the living room and I took the kids upstairs to my bedroom. We played "Spin the Bottle" and then I turned out the lights for some free-lance kissing games. She had on a dark blue velvet dress, Beverly did. While kissing her, I ran my hands all over her dress, even the soft spots in front, and she didn't back off one bit. I got horny as hell. When the party broke up, I took her out to her parents' car and they drove away. But then my crotch hurt like hell. It hurt so much, I puked right there on the grass. When I tried to go back upstairs, I had a 'helluva' time going up those steps. Skipper thought I was clowning around, but I wasn't. I'll always have fond memories of our place in Madras and even Beverly's ranch house way out of town. Will I ever see her again? Who knows? We're like migrant workers, heading for the next apple orchard. Oh, well, tomorrow is another day and all that.

Dad shifts down to second gear as we climb up Cow Canyon and finally come out on a broad rangeland of sagebrush and bunch grass. We cruise past the ghost town of Shaniko and keep rolling north.

Another twenty miles and we come into wheat country. Thousands of acres of wheat on all sides, rising up on small hills and falling back into brushy ravines before rising up again in the distance. We come to the little town of Kent, a cluster of old houses among cottonwood trees and a brick building with a small coffee shop sporting an "open" sign hanging hopefully in the window. This place makes even Madras look good. I remember back when I was twelve, when Mom got me a job in the wheat harvest. Tending header on a combine. Twelve hours a day, hot and noisy and tedious as hell. Mom's idea of "character development." The other crew members were a couple of old guys, friendly and all.

When the boss was gone, they taught me how to sew up sacks of wheat. After supper one night, they told me all about cathouses. Once, when the combine broke down, the Cat-skinner took us on a crazy wild-ass car ride careening around back-country roads—drinking beer and throwing empties out the window—and laughing our stupid heads off. They tried teaching me how to roll cigarettes, but I finally gave up and settled for tailor-mades. I did learn how to smoke without coughing. And I found out that beer has an awful sour taste, but makes everybody laugh and have a good time. If that isn't good character development, what the hell is?

We keep rolling north into more wheat country. A thought comes back to me, something I'd been trying to ignore all day. About that Mexican sonofabitch. Could I escape him this time? By moving to Pendleton? Probably not. He found me when we lived in The Dalles. He found me when we moved to Redmond. He found me when we moved to Madras. So why shouldn't he find me after we move to

Pendleton? How did he do it? Why did he do it? What did he want? What was he after? Did he want to hurt me in some way? If so, why didn't he just stab me when he had the chance?

And those cards! What's that all about? Four of 'em, all spades. Do they mean anything? It's driving me nuts, trying to figure out all this crap and no answers. Nothing, but nothing, makes any sense.

I find an old sweater of mine and roll it into a kind of pillow. I punch it into a spot between the seat and the window and lay my head there. Not bad for a make-do pillow. I shove my head further into the soft yarn and close my eyes. It looks like I'm asleep. Maybe I am, in a half-assed kind of way. Mostly I'm thinking about all the stuff that happened since the day I first saw that Mexican bastard.

We were coming out of a theater in Portland, me and Dad, when I saw him for the first time. He was short and stocky, with black greasy hair and a dark face with a Fu-Manchu moustache. Seems like it happened in a dream, but it was real. Let's see, how old was I then? Six, I think. A little six-year old smart-ass who didn't know what fear was all about. Yeah, I remember. It all started when I was running around crazy in that big old department store...

~ * ~

"Hamilton!"

That was Mom, looking like she was really mad. We were in Meier & Frank, the department store in downtown Portland. It was fifteen stories high, the tallest building in Oregon, and the mecca of all shoppers in the state. And I was riding those crazy moving stairs called escalators up and down the floors.

We had come to the big city from The Dalles, our hometown on the Columbia River, a hundred miles upstream from Portland. After three days of sightseeing, Mom told Dad she was going shopping at Meier & Frank. No big surprise—she had been talking up this store for weeks. My little brother Skipper was two years old, but not able to walk very fast. After dressing him at our hotel, she put him in the stroller. She pushed him, me following, into the elevator and down to the lobby. We went outside, walked the sidewalk for a couple blocks, turned left, crossed the street, followed that sidewalk for a block and suddenly there it was—a gleaming white skyscraper looming high above our heads—Oregon's great temple of commerce, Meier & Frank.

We approached an entrance. Mom opened a heavy glass door and I held it so she could push Skipper's stroller inside. Standing in the front was a man facing us. He was an old guy with a white moustache and white hair, a sharp-looking guy. He was wearing a gray suit with a white shirt, red tie and a red flower in his lapel. I figured he was the governor, for sure, or at least the mayor. If he was a phony big-shot, he sure had me fooled. I thought for sure he was gonna throw us outta there. But he said "good morning" in a friendly way, which was a big relief to me. People were rushing here and there like rabbits in a fire drill. On our left was a row of shiny brass elevators and a lady in a dark green jacket with gold buttons. By her snooty ways, I could tell she was the boss of this place. She kept walking back and forth, clicking a clicker thing and sending people to their elevators. When the Clicker Lady looked at us and pointed to the third elevator, Mom hustled us over there. The door opened and people rushed out. I followed Mom as she pushed Skipper's stroller inside.

I looked at the operator. Younger than the Clicker Lady, she had on a light-blue jacket and dark-blue pants with official-looking stripes down the sides. She wore white gloves and ran the elevator by sliding a brass handle over a half-circle plate. Just like the power control on a ship in a deep-sea movie. And she was just as intent on running her elevator as a captain steering his ocean liner through icebergs in the north Atlantic.

At each floor, she moved the handle to "Stop" and opened the door and called out the stuff they sold on that floor:

Second Floor—Men's Clothing; Third Floor—Women's Clothing
Fourth Floor—Lingerie & Shoes; Fifth Floor—Fabrics & Linens
Sixth Floor—Radios & Sporting Goods
Seventh Floor—Rugs & Draperies; Eighth Floor—Housewares
Ninth Floor—Furniture; Tenth Floor—Georgian Room Restaurant

Mom got off at the third floor and I followed her into Women's Clothing. She headed straight for the stupid dresses and started pawing through the whole pile of them on a rack. A saleslady came over to help, so I saw my chance.

I took off to explore the place. It was kinda funny. Nobody was guarding the escalators like the elevators. I ran over to the escalators, jumped on a step, and took it up one floor to Lingerie & Shoes. I figured out how to circle around, jumped on it again and rode it up to Fabrics & Linens. I found another one going down. I jumped on it, rode three floors down to Men's Clothing, then took another one up to Women's Clothing. That's when I heard Mom yelling my name and knew she was really mad at me. So was the saleslady, an old battleaxe who looked like she wanted to throw me out of a third-floor window.

Mom grabbed me and pushed Skipper's stroller into an elevator. I watched the operator shove the control handle to the store's version of "Full Speed Ahead." Up we went, stopping at each floor, finally reaching the tenth floor. The operator opened the door while Mom pushed Skipper outside. I followed her down a corridor to some fancy restaurant. The hostess led us to a booth near the back, where Mom sat down with a sigh.

Before long, Dad showed up. He was surprised, I think, to be greeted with so much enthusiasm.

"Douglas, thank heaven you're here. I can't shop with Hamilton running wild. You need to take him with you to the baseball game."

"What baseball ga—? Oh, yeah, the baseball game." He took a long time thinking about this. Finally, "Okay, I'll take him with me."

Soon as we finished lunch, Dad paid the bill and told me to come along. We rode the elevator back down and went outside. It was a blue-sky day, perfect for baseball. I thought we would take the streetcar out to the Vaughn Street Ballpark. But it soon hit me that he had some other plans in mind. Was he putting one over on Mom? It sure looked like it. That was a riot, him lying to Mom like that.

We started walking, in a new direction this time. North it was, toward a different part of downtown. We walked for a bunch of blocks, only stopping for red lights at street corners.

We passed a couple of seedy-looking hotels, taverns, and a run-down store with logging boots and work pants. We came to a busy four-lane street and I wondered how we would get across. The light went green and Dad grabbed my hand and we ran across the whole four lanes before the cars came racing through again. He said that was Burnside Street and we were now in the Skid Row part of town. I wasn't sure what Skid Row meant. But I could see it was totally different from the streets around Meier & Frank. We walked a block or two, past guys in shabby coats lined up for food, past other guys sitting in doorways or sleeping on the sidewalk. I wondered why we had come to this sleazy part of town. I wondered where he was taking me.

About a month before this, Mom said we were going on a trip to Portland. I'd been to the big city once before, so I was really pumped up about it. She said Evelyn and Veronica were staying home. That left just me, Dad, Mom, and Skipper. Veronica was six years older than me, and my other sister Evelyn was ten years older.

By this time, I had grown up enough to get some half-assed idea of the world around me. I found out we lived in The Dalles, a town of six thousand people spread over hillsides and little plateaus on the south side of the Columbia River. We lived on Elm Street, in a big old white house with lots of rooms, a full basement and large front porch under cover. Not long after I figured that out, Skipper was born.

I was an ordinary kid with brown hair and no scars or tattoos to pick me out of a police lineup. Dad was six feet tall and lanky, with thin hair and a long face showing his Scottish ancestry. Mom, six years younger and shorter than Dad, had black wavy hair and dark eyebrows, a trace maybe of her family's origins in the Swiss Alps. Evelyn and Veronica were typical teen-agers, slim brunettes wearing sweaters and pleated skirts (or whatever the fashion gods dictated) always chattering about boys or school cliques or hit songs. As for Skipper, he grew into a little kid with sandy hair and a sneaky smile hiding whatever mischief he was cooking up.

When Skipper got older, he followed me around the house all the time, asking me why stuff was this way or that. How was I supposed to know all this stuff? Got here just a few years before he did, for God's sake. I wanted to tell him that, but I figured he was too stupid to get it.

All that junk came a couple of years later. For now, he was okay, just burbling, gurgling and pointing at everything in sight.

A week before the big trip to Portland, Dad came home one night with a brand-new 1935 Studebaker Dictator sedan. It was beautiful. Shiny black, with sweeping lines, streamlined fenders, a swept-wing grill and spare tire kit above the rear bumper. If Hollywood made a movie about some bad guy—say, Pretty Boy Floyd or Machine-Gun Kelly—this would be the car to use. It was said, in fact, that John Dillinger drove a Dictator a couple years earlier during a string of Midwest bank holdups. I doubt if Dad chose the car for that reason. Still, you never know.

When vacation time came, Dad loaded the car trunk with Skipper's stroller and a suitcase, and we climbed aboard. We drove to downtown and took a street that turned into Highway 30 and followed it along a rocky bluff overlooking the river far below. Dad said we were on the Columbia Gorge Highway, and started bragging about it.

"This was the most challenging project in the country when they started back in 1914. Many experts said it couldn't be done, there were too many obstacles. Yet it was built on time and budget, built with men using shovels, dynamite and horse-drawn wagons."

Awesome! Did the contractors make any money?

"Despite all the difficulties, the Gorge Highway has no grade over five percent and no curve radius under one hundred feet."

So what? How am I supposed to know all this crap? That's the trouble with engineers. They always talk like that. Mom told me once when Dad tried to teach her how to drive a stick-shift, he told her to "let out the clutch" when he really wanted her to shove in the clutch pedal. She got so confused she just quit right there on the spot.

Going up on the Rowena Loops, we got behind a big old tanker truck crawling along real slow and filling our car with diesel fumes. I felt sick and told Mom I needed to stop and puke. She said to take some deep breaths. If I could hold it back, she would buy me an ice-cream cone at Crown Point.

Dad rolled his window down and leaned out to see around the truck and fresh air rushed in. It revived me a little. Then he gunned the motor and we took off and passed that stupid tanker-truck like nothing. We sailed along, free at last of those fumes.

I sat back and dreamed about the ice-cream cone. We cruised past the farm village of Mosier and into the Twin Tunnels, along tree-lined bluffs above the river, through the town of Hood River. We kept rolling along a tunnel of trees, past Cascade Locks and Bridge of the Gods, past Horsetail Falls and Multnomah Falls. At Bridal Veil Falls, I could see the wind picking up. Way down below, whitecaps were flying across the whole wide river.

Further on, past Latourell Falls, the wind was really whipping the tree branches around. We came up behind a big lousy box truck, grinding along real slow, climbing the loops to Crown Point. I felt kinda sick again. But then we went around a curve at the top and lost the truck as it headed downhill toward the Sandy River.

"We need to stop here," said Mom.

"We should keep going," said Dad.

"Look. I made a promise to Hamilton. I need to keep it."

I gave Dad a thin little smile, but his expression was grim as he pulled into a parking spot. Perched atop a massive headland, we could see the river for miles east and west. But nobody was looking at the view.

The wind was blowing like a hurricane. With a huge effort, Mom pushed her door open. I tried to force my door, but it felt like pushing a big old grizzly bear. Somehow, I got it open and got out of the car. We struggled to reach the steps of the Vista House. The crazy wind knocked Mom down, but she kept going, crawling up the steps on hands and knees. Then a man helped her get up and opened the big door for us. Inside, it was strangely quiet as the tree branches thrashed around outside. We walked down some marble steps to the lower level and found the snack counter. Mom bought me a chocolate ice cream cone. Promise kept. I happily bit into the ice cream as we climbed back up the steps to the main floor.

Outside, the wind had died down some, so it was easier getting back. Without a word, Dad fired up the car and we drove into the city.

Five Cards and a Cathouse

We went in along Sandy Boulevard, crossed a bridge, and drove into downtown Portland. Plowing through the lousy traffic, we turned left and went into a street loaded with cars, and streets full of people. We turned right, followed some streetcar tracks for several blocks and finally got to a tall brick building. Dad said it was the Rose City Hotel.

We pulled into a parking spot and went inside. Dad lugged the suitcase, Mom carried Skipper, and I had the stupid stroller. We walked up to a counter in the lobby. A guy stood behind there, dressed in a black suit. He had on a bow tie and vest, with a silver chain stretching from one pocket to another, like the sheriff in a Western movie. His head was large and round, with a little patch of black hair parted right down the middle. He wore horn-rimmed glasses with thick lenses, making his eyes loom up larger than life.

"We've got a reservation," said Dad. "The name is Skutt."

The sheriff rummaged through a loose-leaf notebook, turning over the pages several times. He stuck his nose right down in there to see better. "No reservation for a Skutt," he said, pulling on his vest for emphasis.

Dad went ballistic. "I called you people a week ago!" he growled. "What kind of a lousy outfit is this, anyway?"

The sheriff backed off; his big eyes wide with alarm. "WELL! I don't know WHAT to say!" he sputtered, arms waving violently. He jerked his head toward a little guy dressed in a bellboy's uniform. "Andrew!" he yelled. "Where's Miss Wampach?"

Andrew rushed over to the counter. "Miss Wampach went home sick," he said. "Oh, DEAR!" said the sheriff. "NOW what do we do?" He waved both arms around in a circle, hands fluttering like butterflies. His forehead glistened with sweat. He took a hankie out of his coat pocket and wiped his face with a panicky expression. Another grownup retard.

"Look," said Dad. "Do you have any rooms available?"

The sheriff ran his finger along a plastic diagram. He put his nose right down on the plastic. "Oh, YES!" he cried, with utter relief. "We have TWO ROOMS left! Only problem is, they're both in front, facing Yamhill. Most people don't—

"It's okay," said Dad. "We'll take one of those in front."

"Oh, WONDERFUL," said the sheriff. He suddenly turned into a figure of fierce authority. "Andrew!" he barked. "Take these folks up to their room." Andrew took the key and led us to the elevator. He took us up to the third floor and down the hallway.

Our room was overlooking Yamhill Avenue. Once inside, I just stood there at the window soaking up the sights and sounds. Especially the streetcars screeching along the tracks, sparks flying from the overhead lines.

That first night in Portland, we saw a movie called *The Scarlett Pimpernel,* with Leslie Howard, at a theater called the Orpheum. It was one of several movie houses along Portland's entertainment street called—what else? —Broadway. Going inside the Orpheum was a special treat. Once past the bright lights and glittering box office, we entered a hushed magical palace with deep carpets, heavy drapes and a special smell reeking of opulence and grandeur.

Usher girls in shiny blue uniforms held little flashlights and helped guide us to our seats. After sitting down, I looked around at the crazy walls and ceilings, a dazzling bonanza of back-lit sculptures and statues. There was so much phony stuff to stare at, I wondered if anyone watched the movie show. No problem. Once the lights dimmed and the musical fanfare blasted away and the curtains parted, all eyes were riveted on the big screen.

The next night we saw *The Thin Man,* with William Powell and Myrna Loy, at the Fox Theater. We could've seen this same movie back home in The Dalles. But it seemed a thousand times more thrilling to join the throngs of ritzy theater-goers outside and follow them into the movie palace, with those smiling girls in shiny satin costumes showing us to our seats.

Those first days in Portland, we rode streetcars everywhere. Over the Willamette River and east on Division Street out to Mt. Tabor park and back. North on Interstate Avenue out to Jantzen Beach and back. South on Macadam clear out to Lake Oswego and back. One morning we took a streetcar from someplace near Multnomah Stadium. It climbed up and up—like the Little Engine That Could—past houses growing bigger and grander as we moved higher and higher up through Portland Heights to the very top of Council Crest. During a brief stop, we walked around the little park. We looked through gaps in the tall fir trees, north toward Mt. St. Helens and then east toward the Cascades foothills rising up into the shining white cone of Mt. Hood.

That afternoon we split up. Mom took Skipper to the hotel. Dad took me on a streetcar out to the Vaughn Street Ballpark. He got the tickets and we went inside. It was an old wooden grandstand, with stupid posts all over holding up the roof. Luckily, we didn't have to twist our heads around a post to see the field. We watched the Portland Beavers play the San Francisco Seals.

We walked past guys lying on the sidewalk and others asleep in doorways. Some were standing around and others just sitting on the stupid curb holding paper sacks with bottles inside. We crossed a street and walked by another seedy-looking hotel. Then we came to the Star Theater.

Dad walked up to the creepy box office and bought tickets from an old guy half-asleep. We walked over to a rusty metal door and went inside.

This theater wasn't anything like those movie palaces a few blocks uptown. The lobby had a threadbare old carpet with a musty smell. The walls were painted plywood covered with old movie posters. I followed Dad to an archway and we pushed through some shabby curtains. It was even worse inside where the audience sat, with bleak house lights, rows of patched-up seats and a grubby floor. And no smiling girl ushers in shiny satin uniforms, for sure.

We had to pick our own seats, but Dad didn't seem to mind. He seemed real happy, happier than usual, I thought. He dropped into his seat with a smile and motioned me to take the seat next to him.

Upfront, below the stage, was a crew-cut guy with drums and cymbals. Suddenly he belted out a drum roll and hit the cymbals with his stick. The house lights went out, the curtains opened and a spotlight picked out a little fat man up on the stage. He swung his cane, tipped his straw hat to the crowd and tap-danced across the stage. There was a ripple of applause. The fat man took off his hat and bowed. He tried to put it back on his head, but stuck it on his cane. Looking around for his hat, he saw it on the cane. He grabbed for it. But it was out of reach. He lunged at it, desperately trying to grab the hat. But he couldn't catch it, no matter how hard he tried.

The crowd roared. They were all men, totally out of control. Two of them, sitting three rows ahead of us, playfully punched each other with good-natured laughs. Dad was laughing, too, more than I had ever seen him laugh. I felt a sense of pleasure myself. It was fun being there with him, being one of the guys watching this show and fitting in with whatever was going on.

The little fat man stood on the stage looking at the audience. I could see he was gonna tell a joke. I could see it by the way he twirled his cane and tugged at his coat lapels.

"Why is your wife like your old Packard?" he barked out. Not a sound broke the silence. The guys were grinning at each other, waiting for the punch line. "Just when you need her, she won't turn over!"

The drum guy hit his cymbals and the crowd erupted. Dad was laughing, too, laughing like crazy. I didn't get the joke. But I forced a laugh anyway. The little fat man pulled on his coat lapels and leaned forward.

"A single man gets home, sees what's in the fridge, and goes to bed. A married man comes home, sees what's in bed, and goes to the fridge."

The cymbals clanged and everybody laughed. Now I was getting the hang of it. When he tells a joke, I told myself, wait for the cymbals to clang. Then laugh out loud. Laugh like crazy.

"What's the difference between bigamy and monogamy?"

Again, silence waiting for an answer. "There's no difference. With bigamy, you've got one wife too many. Same thing with monogamy. One wife too many."

Again, the cymbals clanged. I laughed out loud, along with Dad and the others. So what if I didn't get the joke? What did it matter? The little fat man ran off the stage. Nothing happened for a moment. Some sinister-sounding music started coming out of the speakers.

Then a lady appeared onstage, the most beautiful lady I had ever seen. She was tall and thin, with long black hair, dressed in a red velvet gown that came down to the floor. She walked slowly across the stage, like a princess. She stopped and gazed at the crowd with a kind of snooty manner. I looked around at the audience. No laughter now. Men gaped in wonder and astonishment, like they had never seen such a sight. Dad was serious, too, watching her every move.

She walked with a stately and deliberate manner back to the center of the stage. Carefully, she reached up and unhooked a button at the top of her dress. The silence was thick and heavy. Slowly and carefully, she pulled the zipper in front all the way down. She stepped out of the gown, clad only in lacy negligee and high heels. She kicked the gown away as if kicking away any trace of modesty. It was shocking. Unbelievable. It was thrilling. There was a stir in the audience, a sort of collective longing.

"Take it off!" yelled an old man sitting up on the front row. I was shocked to hear him yell like that. I couldn't believe he would say that. As for me, I didn't know what to do—whether to stare or cover my eyes. The drummer was no help. He just sat there and stared like everyone else. I had nothing to go on except look at Dad and listen to that scary music.

She walked around the stage with that regal bearing. All I could think of was the princess in a fairy tale. Only I had never seen a princess in high heels and negligee, even in a fairy tale book. She walked slowly around, now and then stopping to give the audience that snooty look. The solemn faces in the audience followed her every move. Suddenly she stopped. With one swift move, she pulled off her negligee and flung it away. I was shocked, more than ever, to see her standing there in nothing but panties and bra, disdainfully looking at the crowd. She turned and walked again, slowly and with great majesty, her hips moving in a slightly exaggerated way, around and around the stage. Then she stopped and looked straight at the audience.

"Take it off!" yelled the old man upfront. All the other guys just sat there, looking on with a kind of reverence, silently begging for the next step. Then she whirled around, black hair flying. With her back to the audience, she unbuckled her bra and threw it away. The crowd groaned, a collective pleading to turn around. But the spotlight winked out and she ran off the stage and the curtains closed. The little fat man ran out on the stage.

"Gorgeous women don't bother me," he said and waited a second. "I wish they would!" The cymbals clanged and the audience roared with laughter. I was so overcome with some new feeling I forgot to laugh. I couldn't get my mind off that lady in red. Strange new sensations churned around inside me. It wasn't like I was mad at anybody. But I wasn't very comfortable either. So I gave up trying to figure out what was happening to me. I took in a couple of deep breaths, like Mom said, when I needed to puke.

The little fat man continued. "A couple go to a hotel. This is Kentucky, horse country. He tells the clerk they just got married. 'You want the bridal?' asks the clerk. The man thinks about it. 'Naw, I'll just grab her by the ears 'til she gets the hang of it!'"

The cymbals clanged, the crowd laughed and I laughed harder than anyone else. I had no idea what I was laughing about, but at least I was keeping up with all the other guys and that made me happy.

As the program went on, two other ladies—a redhead in a green outfit, and a blonde in a shiny black gown—went through the same routine. Each time, the same deal. Each of them walked around the stage in that snooty way, each unzipped her gown and walked around in her negligee. Each of them threw away the negligee and walked around in panties and bra. Each time, the men watched with high hopes as the lady turned her back to the crowd and undid her bra. Each time, they looked on, crestfallen, as the spotlight went out and the curtains closed as she ran offstage. Watching this, I could understand my own feelings a little bit better. I even liked the stupid music. It didn't seem so sinister anymore. It seemed kinda exciting in some strange new way.

After the blonde lady ran offstage, the little fat man came through the curtains and onto the stage in front. He told more jokes and I laughed as hard as I could whenever the drummer hit the cymbals. I was really happy, being Dad's buddy and now a jaded veteran of burlesque shows. It made me feel like a real grownup man-of-the-world.

The little fat man said something, gave a deep bow and ran off the stage as the house lights came back on. There was a ripple of applause as everybody stood up and got ready to leave. I stood up, too, and waited for Dad as he sidled down the row of seats. We walked up the aisle, through the archway curtains and out of the crappy little lobby.

We shuffled outside with the other men, some wearing hats pulled down over their eyes, making our way back to the real world. Outside, there were some shabby guys hanging around the sidewalk. One of them, a guy sitting on a car fender, jumped to his feet when he saw us. He looked to me like a Mexican—short and stocky and dark skin with a Fu Manchu moustache and greasy black hair. He took a step, stopped and watched us go down the street, then started walking a short distance behind us.

"Dad!" I whispered. "That guy is following us!"

"What guy?" he asked, looking around. "There's a whole bunch of men behind us."

"The Mexican guy. The one with the moustache."

"Oh, it's that imagination of yours," he said with a smile. "You'll soon forget about it—like everything else you saw today. Okay?"

"Okay." We came to Burnside Street. Just as before, Dad waited for the green light, then grabbed my hand and pulled me across the four lanes before traffic came roaring by again. I looked across the street. Sure enough, there was the Mexican, standing on the curb watching us. I thought he would run across at the next green light. But—surprise! —he turned and went back toward the Star Theater. I was safe! He wasn't trying to come after me! I was so happy, I skipped along like a little kid instead of taking solemn steps like a real man. But my stupid heart was pounding like crazy as we walked back to the bright and respectable part of town.

When we got back to the hotel, I said zero-nothing to Mom about where we had been. I remembered Dad's instructions and for once had enough sense to keep my big mouth shut. That evening, we strolled along Broadway, Mom pushing Skipper in the stroller and Dad happily smoking a cigar. After some window-shopping, we went to a restaurant for dinner. The next day, our vacation week was finished. Dad met with the sheriff and paid the hotel bill. Then we loaded up the Studebaker and took off. We drove through downtown Portland, across the Willamette River and east out Sandy Boulevard to Troutdale. We followed Highway 30 along the Sandy River, climbed the highlands to Crown Point and headed back home along the Columbia Gorge Highway.

Back in The Dalles. I couldn't get that Mexican guy out of my mind. Why did he jump up when he saw us? Why did he look at me that way? Why did he follow us? All this crazy stuff went round and round in my head, while I tried to forget it. Gradually, I did kinda forget about it as I got back to regular life and ordinary stuff. I just hoped we lived far enough from Portland that he couldn't find me back here in The Dalles.

Dad's job made him responsible for keeping all the state highways in good shape in all directions. That was Highway 30 running east to Arlington and west to Cascade Locks, plus Highway 97 going south for about sixty miles. I went along a couple times on inspection trips, so I got to see how it worked. Highway 97 was a no-brainer. From Biggs Junction south, it was an ordinary two-lane highway running through wheat country and some high-range desert.

Not much could happen to this highway except maybe some potholes here and there. When there were enough potholes to bother with, Dad sent some guys out in a gravel truck with hot asphalt and a steamroller. It was usually sunny weather, not much traffic, and so quiet you could hear a meadowlark sing. If a car or truck came along, the driver just stopped and waited for the steamroller to roll the patch. Nobody ever seemed to be in a big hurry. One of the truckers might get out and jaw with the highway crew, who probably enjoyed the company. It was different on Highway 30, the Columbia Gorge Highway, the one we took on the trip to Portland. When it was finished in 1922, Dad said they called it poetry in stone. They compared it with scenic highways in Europe, a string of tunnels and bridges forging a paved road over the high crests and steep forested slopes of the Columbia

River Gorge. Designed for leisurely travel, it was a two-lane scenic parkway lined with stonewall guard rails, set like stone jigsaw puzzles, in retaining walls and arched ramparts overlooking the wide river far below.

By the thirties, however, it carried tons of traffic. The highway was a major route for big trucks and buses and thousands of cars each day. Falling rocks were a big problem, especially in the winter. Sometimes a whole hillside came roaring down in a huge avalanche that buried the road. Once in a while, it buried motorists. That was called a slide. One thing that Dad really feared was a slide on the Columbia Gorge Highway.

But snow was still the main enemy. One winter brought a storm that shut down the highway for a whole week. Everybody was in full panic to get it open. Dad sent out all the snow-plow crews and snow-blower crews he could find. He scraped the bottom of the barrel, that's for sure. Some of them were greenhorns, maybe, or they were scummy guys who didn't give a darn. Near Cascade Locks, the highway ran parallel to the Union Pacific Railroad. One day, a crew blew a bunch of snow over the side and onto the railroad tracks. Soon the "City of Portland" streamliner train came flying in from Chicago, wheels pounding the rails at seventy miles an hour. Going around a curve, the engineer saw the snow and pulled the brakes and the trains skidded a half-mile before grinding to a halt just short of the big snow pile.

It wasn't long before the Union Pacific President called the Oregon governor who called the Highway Commission who called the director of the Highway Department who called—well, when Dad reached over to pick up his phone, you can bet it was smoking. How he kept his head off the chopping block is anyone's guess.

Two

"*Velkommen!*"

Velkommen. That killed me. It sounded like "welcome" in a weird kind of way. That was our next-door neighbor. He and his wife lived in this dark-green house with white trim and window boxes full of flowers. It looked like one of those gingerbread houses in fairy tales. Like the one where Little Red Riding Hood finds a wolf dressed up like her grandma.

Mom said they were Germans, whatever that was. I didn't see much of the old lady. She just hung around the kitchen, I guess, cooking up whatever Germans like to eat. But the old guy, he was always outside, watering the flowers or pushing a lawnmower over their little patch of grass. He was pretty active for a fat old guy. I liked to go over there on Sundays. They took a different paper than we did, so I went over there to look at their funnies.

I just walked up on their front porch and rang the doorbell. The old guy came to the door. "*Velkommen!*" he said. "How *ist die mutter? Unt der vader? Unt der bruder? Unt die schwesters?*" "Okay." I knew he meant Mom and Dad and the others, but he sounded really weird talking like that.

His name was Mr. Fenstermacher and he was always smoking one of those pipes that start at your mouth, curl around down under your chin and come back up to the open end. He was always blowing air through the pipe or stuffing in tobacco or lighting it with a kitchen match or drawing in a big breath and blowing out a cloud of smoke. His whole house smelled of smoke and he was pretty smoky himself.

"Vel, do you vant der funnies?" he asked as I came inside. Vel, do I vant der funnies? Of course, I vant der funnies. Why can't he talk American like everybody else? I nodded.

He shuffled over, got his paper, pulled out the funnies and brought them over to me. I spread them out on the dining room table and climbed up on a chair to take a look. I couldn't read yet, so I just looked at the characters doing crazy stuff.

"You like der funnies? *Ist gute*, yah?"

Ist gute, yah? How could I talk with this guy? I just looked at him and nodded. He was sitting over there on his couch, in some old pants with red suspenders and old plaid shirt, smoking his big pipe. He was kinda gross, if you want to know the truth. He was really fat, as I said, and he had a big nose with little hairs coming out of the end. His face had red lumps all over it and he kinda drooled when he took his pipe out of his mouth. But he was a nice old guy, even if he grossed me out sometimes.

When I finished with the funnies, I jumped down off the chair. "Thank you, Mr. Fenstermacher," I said, just like Mom told me.

"*Bitte schon*," he said, smiling and nodding. "Unt come back venever you vish." He opened the front door. "Mit der little bruder if you vish."

Venever you vish? Mit der little bruder? I nodded, waved goodbye, walked down his steps and along the sidewalk back home. Venever you vish? I couldn't get that out of my head.

Our place on Elm Street was a big old white house with covered porch and steps leading down to a lawn with an oak tree. It was a great place for playing with other kids. We roamed all over the neighborhood, one block over to Bluff Street and two blocks east and west from there. We ran around that open zone all day long, free as birds, nobody saying we had to quit for some reason, looking for adventure and sometimes finding it.

Our house had a one-car garage, a garden and lots of grass. It even had a rain barrel and a cellar door. All this came with two sisters who liked to brew up stuff to drink.

Like root beer. I saw an old Prohibition movie once, with some moonshine stills out in the boondocks. That's just what it looked like in our basement—jugs full of murky slop and loops of copper tubes running from one jug to another. All this to make root beer. It didn't make any sense. Dad could've bought them tons of the stuff if they had asked. But, no, they had to make it with their own little hands. To keep me out of it, Evelyn told me they stirred it with a stick covered with manure. Yuck! I wouldn't go near the brew after that.

One day Evelyn invited her new boyfriend home for dinner. He came in, all dressed up in a jazzy sports jacket, shirt and bow tie, slacks, and a dazzling pair of white buck shoes. He patted me on the head to show how nice and friendly he was. A real phony jerk, sure, but I could see he was my kind of guy. Not finicky or squeamish, just sensitive and discriminating. Like me.

After shaking hands with Dad, he wiped his hands on his pants. Good idea. At the table, he checked his fork to see if it was clean. Good idea. Then he took a napkin and wiped it around the rim of his drinking glass. Good idea.

Mom brought out spaghetti and meatballs and lots of salad. Everybody was happy as moles in a mushroom farm. Mom gave Skipper a little plate of spaghetti which he tried to eat. Evelyn went into the kitchen and came marching back with a big pitcher of her root beer. Mom got me a glass of milk. Evelyn was beaming at her boyfriend, hoping he was duly impressed. She poured him some root beer. "I made this myself," she said proudly.

He seemed to be having a good time. Napkin tucked under his chin, he wolfed down some spaghetti and speared a meatball or two. Then he took his glass of root beer and socked away a long swig of the stuff. He looked at me. "Why aren't you drinking Evelyn's root beer'!" he asked, just before taking another big swallow.

"'Cause she stirred it with a manure stick."

His neck jerked back and he coughed and sprayed root beer all over the table. He went into a coughing fit until Dad whacked him on the back. Then he staggered to his feet, stumbled out the front door and we never saw him again. My kind of guy. Sensitive and discriminating.

~ * ~

Among the neighborhood kids was a girl named Sylvia Gardner. By now, I had decided that girls were okay after all. Odd little creatures, sure, but fun to be around in some weird sort of way. I called her "old Sylvia" by way of our friendship.

That's what we called our friends—"old Jack" or "old Peggy"— like "good old Bill" or "good old Barbara." Old Sylvia lived in a light-blue house half-a-block toward Bluff Street.

She was sorta cute, with dark eyes and curly brown hair. I was at her house one day. Suddenly she got up and walked to the staircase.

"Come on upstairs," she said. "I want to show you something."

"What is it?"

"It's a surprise. You'll see."

This was kinda exciting, so I followed her upstairs. "Come into my bedroom," she said. I followed her inside, feeling a strange thrill.

She walked over to a bay window and stood by a three-story model house. It was huge, red with white trim, with a wrap-around porch, windows, chimneys and little shingles on the roof—the whole works.

"Isn't it beautiful?" she exclaimed. "I got it for my birthday. It's the most beautiful doll house in the world. Look, it's even got furniture inside that you can move around from the back."

As she said this, she got behind it and pushed some tiny chairs to show me. Yes, it was okay. But I got that tingling feeling again. While she was raving on about that stupid dollhouse, I kept looking at her bed. I kept thinking about getting in and rolling around in bed with her. It was a weird feeling, confusing and exciting.

"What do you think about it?" she asked suddenly.

"I think it would be lotsa fun!"

"What? What do you mean?"

"Oh, the dollhouse! To have a dollhouse like this. Lotsa fun." That seemed a good answer.

"C'mon," she said and walked out of the bedroom. As we went downstairs, she had no idea what I was thinking. I wasn't too sure myself.

~ * ~

Since I had reached the ripe old age of six, I was old enough to start school. That September, Mom enrolled me in the first grade. To reach the grade school, I had to go one block over to Bluff Street, then walk east five blocks to the school. This detour was necessary since Elm Street was a dead-end. It came to a halt two blocks short of the school. Somehow this bothered me. I figured it should go all the way through. One morning, I decided to blaze a new trail. At the end of Elm Street, I set off into the unknown wilderness. I climbed over fences, scrambled through backyards, ducked under clothes-lines and plowed through gardens. Finally, I climbed another fence and—eureka! —I was in the school playground! I was Columbus! I was Lewis and Clark! I was late.

Entering the first-grade room, I hoped to sneak in and just sit at my desk. But the eagle-eyed Miss Borkowski stopped me in my tracks.

"Hamilton!"

"Yes, Miss Borkowski?"

"Come up here."

I took the long walk up there, all the way to the front.

"Do you know what time it is?" I shook my head.

"It's twenty minutes past the hour. You are twenty minutes late." I knew it was hopeless to explain about the exciting new route I had blazed, so I just stood there. Miss Borkowski was a heavy woman, a very heavy woman. She had heavy legs and heavy arms and heavy bosom. She had a heavy face with heavy eyebrows and a heavy dose of rouge on her heavy cheeks. Her voice was heavy and deep and she looked like a logger dolled up in a dress and wig for a Halloween party.

"Bend over and grab your ankles, Hamilton."

I knew what that meant. A good whipping with that stainless-steel yardstick she kept under her desk.

"This will hurt me more than you," she said.

Yeah, right, I thought. Then she wound up and came back with two whacks on my butt. One and then another. Two whacks. Not too bad, if you want the truth. Not like Dad's home-run hits, that's for sure. I think she pulled her punches at the last second. But they drew an appreciative "awwwww" from the audience. Two whacks.

"All right, Hamilton. You may go back to your desk now."

I took the long walk back, avoiding the eyes of my classmates. Especially Sylvia, who wanted me to succeed in this grade school business.

"Let that be a lesson to you," declared Miss Borkowski to the class. "The kind of student we want to avoid being is just like Hamilton. Let him be an example to you. A horrible example, in fact."

Thus began my career as Horrible Example, an honor I accepted with modesty and humility. In the days after, I kept using my secret new route and kept going in late and kept getting spanked. Then my secret new route became commonplace and wasn't fun anymore. So I went back to the old Bluff Street route and got to school on time.

As for the lessons, I had trouble understanding what it was all about. Sylvia Gardner was the star of the class. She was always the first one to shoot up her hands with the right answer. Old Sylvia tried to help me, but I just couldn't get it. Like, one plus one makes two. Two plus two makes four was really going off the deep end. With reading, we had to learn the vowels—the "a" and "e" sounds and the rest—then we had to learn the consonants, like exploding your lips for the "b" sound or humming to make the "m" sound.

It was a tough grind, but Sylvia kept me working on it. I finally got so I could read a little bit—a triumph so great she gave me a pat on the back. That was a huge reward and it kept me working on it. Eventually, I became such a great scholar that I could read the little book that Miss Borkowski handed out.

The book had a story line I could follow. "See Dick," it read. "See Dick Run." Okay, I got that. "Run, Dick, Run." Okay, I got that too. But what if Dick stopped running? Did that mean I had to learn a bunch of new words? That was a scary thought.

One good thing about the first grade. No homework, so evenings were free to enjoy the radio programs. After dinner, Dad always pulled the curtains shut and turned on our big dark-brown Philco floor radio. Then he turned the dial to run the pointer across the yellow light to the magic spot for our favorite radio program.

As he did this, we pulled up chairs in a semi-circle and stared at the velvet speakers. Each night brought a new show, another version from the previous week. We listened to *I Love A Mystery* and *Manhattan Merry-Go-Round* and one that came on with machine-gun fire, sirens and a deep voice announcing *Gang Busters*. The Lone Ranger theme set off new adventures of the wandering cowboy and his Indian sidekick Tonto, riding the Old West to save the innocent and punish the guilty. Those thrilling stories of yesteryear came with the galloping crescendos of the William Tell Overture and the hero's cry of "Hi yo, Silver!" Hot stuff.

My favorite show, *The Shadow*, was about a mysterious crime fighter who fought bad guys by making himself invisible. I shivered each time I heard that spooky organ music and chilling laugh and that menacing voice: "Who knows what evil lurks in the hearts of men? The Shadow knows!" The announcer said the Shadow was "Lamont Cranston, wealthy young man-abouttown, whose hobby is bringing crooks to justice."

Lamont Cranston became my role model in a stupid kind of way. He aroused a kind of fantasy in me. I wanted to be just like him. It wasn't about chasing crooks. No, leave that to the cops. My fantasy was having a name like Lamont Cranston and being a wealthy young man-about-town. But how could you be a wealthy young man-about-town in The Dalles? Where do you go for the night life? There were some cruddy taverns on the main street. When Mom took me downtown for grocery shopping, we walked by some taverns—black holes belching jukebox country songs and sour smells—not much fun there. Or maybe I could join the Elks Club. But they'd soon get tired of me and vice-versa. What I needed was a big city like Portland. What I needed was tons of money and a big city with lots of night clubs to show off my Lamont Cranston routine. In the meantime, all I could do was wait to grow up, go to movies and listen to the radio.

Fibber McGee and Molly had a phony old windbag and his wife living at 79 Wistful Vista. Each week, we waited for Fibber to open his closet door, with sounds of stuff falling out—a scene long enough to empty a dozen closets—as we laughed our heads off. Each week brought a new get-rich-quick scheme which failed miserably and another verbal brawl with Fibber's next-door neighbor, the Great Gildersleeve.

Radio brought on the idea of popular hit songs. Veronica always wanted to be up-to-date on these and often brought home new sheet music. We had an upright piano of dark walnut with a matching bench. Mom could play the piano, so she got drafted into trying out each new song. She played the melody okay, but her beat was dry and virtuous like a hymn. Sometimes Evelyn brought home the record so we could hear the way it was supposed to sound—songs like "Lovely To Look At," "Just One Of Those Things," "There's A Small Hotel," and "Goody Goody."

One of the first movies I saw was 7*Public Enemy* with James Cagney smashing a grapefruit on his girlfriend's face. Johnny Weissmuller, as Tarzan the Ape Man, had a blood-curdling call that could stampede a herd of elephants. At first, I couldn't understand why he had that jungle yell. But in the next movie, he had the beautiful Jane in her short little tunic gazing up at him in total rapture. I could see right away that advertising paid off big, even in the jungle.

We saw some scary movies with a werewolf named Lon Chaney and guys with weird foreign accents, like Bela Lugosi in *Dracula* and Boris Karloff in *Frankenstein*. I liked the comedies most of all. Laurel and Hardy were funny when fixing a house, swinging lumber around and clobbering each other. W. C. Fields was a guy with a big nose and squinty eyes. As a rent-a-cop in The Bank Dick, he grabs a little kid wearing a cowboy outfit and snatches his cap gun away. There was a movie called *Modern Times* with Charlie Chaplin as a factory worker trying to keep up with an assembly line going faster and faster. It was funny and sad at the same time.

Sometimes I wondered about all this. Sometimes I wondered what kind of life it was around here before radio and movies. What did those poor saps do all that time? How did they keep from going nuts, just looking at each other's stupid faces and their four blank walls all day long?

I chummed around sometimes with a kid named Gary Stratton. He lived in an unpainted house on Bluff Street. Old Stratton had stringy blond hair and sleepy eyes. He was curious about everything and always dragged me into it. We roamed the neighborhood, looking for something exciting to mess with. Once we found a shabby old billboard lying face-down in a vacant lot.

"Help me dig this out," Stratton said.

"What for? What's the idea?"

"We need to find out what it says. Maybe it's got a treasure map." That made sense to me. So we got shovels and started digging it out from underbrush and solid dirt. We worked on it for two days.

After we cleared off the brush and dug the frame out, we got some ropes and tied them to the corners. With lots of heaving and grunting, we finally pulled the stupid billboard over. The sign was caked with dirt, so we got a pail of water and some old towels to wash it off. After more hours of washing off all the dirt, we could finally see the original sign.

The billboard was advertising cigarettes. There was a big picture of a woman with short black hair and a straight dress, waving a cigarette in a holder. The artwork looked like sheet music from the twenties. That made it really old, like something out of King Tut's tomb. Stratton bent down over the sign for a closer look. He pointed to some hand printing near the bottom of the sign. It was in big black letters, written with a Crayola.

"Look!" he said, all excited. "It's some kind of secret message! If we could read it, maybe we could find a hidden treasure!"

Both of us were having problems learning to read. Now I understood why Miss Borkowski was so anxious to get it through our heads. If only we could read, we could figure out important messages like this one. I tried hard to remember the sounds of each letter and to put those sounds together. This was my first time reading something outside class. The message started with an "f" so I started from there.

I sounded out the letter, blowing air between my lower lip and upper teeth. Then I tried the rest of it, starting with the "u" sound. It came out as "fu" and closed with the clicking sound from "k" or "c"—"fuck"—and then I worked on the second word. It started with the "y" letter followed by two letters "o" and "u" making the "ooooo" sound—"fuck you"—I had read my first sentence in the real world!

"It says fuck you," I told Stratton. He just shrugged. He didn't know what it meant and neither did I. So we just forgot about it.

Old Stratton was always wondering what fantastic treasures were out there waiting to be found. He harped on this so much, he got me hooked into thinking that way, too.

One day we heard about an old TB hospital that was shut down. It sounded like a perfect place to explore and maybe find some treasure. They said it was located on a hilltop above town, on a grassy ridge just beyond the cherry orchards. They said you could find it by following a gravel road starting at the end of a paved road near our school. In the afternoon, right after school, we set out to find that old TB hospital.

We hiked up the paved road to the end and followed the gravel road as it climbed up and up, winding through endless forests of cherry trees. Finally, we got tired and sat on an old log at a driveway. Then Stratton looked at a bottle of milk sitting underneath a mailbox. He jumped up and grabbed a smooth rock and tossed it to me.

"Betcha can't hit that milk bottle," he said.

"What? You wanna get me in trouble?"

"C'mon! You're chicken, that's what!"

"Yeah? Well, you do it then! Unless you're chicken—"

With that, he picked up another rock from the ground. He stood up and fired the rock. It hit the bottle square and smashed it into a million pieces of glass, with milk running all over the ground.

"That was fun!" he said. "Let's find another one!"

I had to admit, it was fun. We walked up the road, faster this time, and came to another driveway. It was the same setup: mailbox on a post and bottle of milk right below. I picked up a nice round rock, took a breath, and fired away—missed. I picked up another rock and fired away—it hit! The bottle smashed with a big crash and milk ran all over the road.

"Boy, was that fun!" cried Stratton, pounding me on the back. We kept hiking up the gravel road, but didn't find any more driveways. We kept walking, looking for mailboxes. We were so intent on our mission, we didn't notice that light was draining from the sky. Finally, the sun set. Everything got dark. It was so dark you could hardly see the edge of the road. Then we saw the lights of a car coming.

"It's a cop car!" yelled Stratton. The car slowed down, came up beside us and stopped. The cop got out and walked over, pointing a big flashlight at us. He asked who we were. We were too scared to lie, I guess, and gave him our names. He told us to get in the car. As we climbed in the back, I just knew we were going to jail for the rest of our lives. But the cop said my mom had called in when I didn't show up after school and he had been out looking for us. Stratton and I just looked at each other and sank back in relief.

Then the cop took us home. That was it. Neither one of us got taken to the police station to get fingerprinted or shoved around by the cops. He just took us home. And we never even got spanked. I guess nobody found out about our crime, except those who went down to get their milk. Later, I got to thinking about it. I felt real guilty, to tell the truth. What if some little baby had diphtheria and died because it didn't have any milk? What if somebody's old grandpa got a stroke and died because there was no milk? In a way, I wished that cop had cuffed us around and thrown us in jail for a week. Then I wouldn't feel so bad about it. Maybe Stratton didn't feel that way, but I did.

~ * ~

Each Sunday morning, I grabbed the funnies from our paper and checked them out. I got so I could read some of the words and it was more fun than just looking at the stupid drawings.

It wasn't too bad figuring out the action in *Barney Google and The Gumps* and *The Katzenjammer Kids*. In *Gasoline Alley,* there was an old guy named Uncle Walt. Somebody left a little baby boy on his doorstep and he named it Skeezix. As the years went by, the kid grew up just like everybody else.

The craziest strip was *Alley Oop*, a caveman riding around on his dinosaur Dinny in the woods and swamps of dinosaur times. After I had learned to read better, I soaked up other comics like *Terry and the Pirates* and *Blondie*. I liked the Popeye strip about the one-eyed sailor, along with his girlfriend Olive Oyl and his best friend, Wimpy. My favorite cop was Dick Tracy, who took on the bad guys like Flattop and Pruneface.

Then a new comic appeared. It was called *Li'l Abner* and it blew me away. It was much better than *Popeye*. It was about some hillbillies in a place called Dogpatch somewhere in Appalachia. There was Li'l Abner's girlfriend, Daisy Mae—much better than pencil-thin Olive Oyl—and his Mammy and Pappy Yokum. There were characters like Marryin' Sam and Earthquake McGoon and Hairless Joe, brewer of Kickapoo Joy Juice. Joe Btfsplk, a guy of good intentions spread disaster wherever he went. The hottest ladies around town were Moonbeam McSwine and Stupefyin' Jones.

With movies, *The Trail of the Lonesome Pine* was my first color film. The scenery is great with big pine trees and a lake by the family cabin. It's someplace in Appalachia, the same as Dogpatch. Only these hillbillies are different. Henry Fonda is the local hick, and he seems lots smarter than Li'l Abner. But he can't get to first base with his wannabe girlfriend. She has the hots for a big-city mining engineer, Fred MacMurray, who is working to bring in the railroad for a mining scheme.

Fonda's family and another clan have been feuding for a hundred years and nobody can stop it. They're always taking pot-shots at each other, so you wonder how any work gets done. A kid, Spanky McFarland, hangs around Fred MacMurray and some other guy operating a steam-shovel on the railroad grade. Once the kid climbs up in the steam-shovel when it's parked on a bridge. I thought he might start the engine and get in big trouble. Instead, the other clan sets off some dynamite which kills the kid. That does it for Henry Fonda. He takes off and marches right over to the enemy's cabin. He tells them it's time to end the feud. The old boss agrees to this. But when Fonda leaves, he gets shot in the back by the boss's son, who in turn gets shot by the boss. That finishes off Fonda and leaves his wannabe girlfriend free to marry Fred MacMurray.

Dad never read any books…maybe an engineering article in a highway magazine. Sometimes he picked up a *Life* magazine before dinner. But Mom was always working through a book. She joined some phony club that sent books in the mail. A new one arrived each month, so she had to finish the old book before the new one came. Like Charlie Chaplin on the assembly line. She read novels by Ernest Hemingway, Sinclair Lewis and some others. Then along came a book that hit like a bombshell.

The book was *Lost Horizon* by James Hilton. It's about some people on an airliner that crash-lands in the Himalayas. All the passengers are rescued. They are taken to a Tibetan monastery in a hidden valley called Shangri-La. The place is totally peaceful and without any problems, a paradise on earth. The hero, an English diplomat, wants to stay there forever. But another guy, a crazy American, prowls around like a caged tiger trying to escape. All of them finally do leave, which shows how stupid people can be.

Mom really got hooked on this story. She wanted Dad to read the book, but he decided to wait for the movie. Sure enough, Hollywood came out with one. It was black-and-white, with lots of snow, a huge big monastery and Tibetan monks all over the place. Mom said the scenery was just like she imagined and the lead actor, Ronald Coleman, was perfect. Dad just smiled in a smug way, as if to say: "See, I didn't need to read the book after all."

I got blown away by a movie called *Snow White and The Seven Dwarfs*. It was an animation in full color and lasted as long as a real movie. Each of the seven dwarfs has a unique personality, like Grumpy, Happy and Bashful, and they work together in a mine. Snow White finds their little cabin in the woods and moves in with them. She is hiding out from the queen, her wicked stepmother. The queen likes to look in her mirror and say, "Mirror, mirror, on the wall. Who is fairest of them all?"

Are you kidding me? She is old and ugly with an evil look. Of course, the queen knows she's not hot stuff. That's why she's jealous of Snow White...for being so young and beautiful. That's why she sends forest rangers out to find her and bring her back. And that's why she cons Snow White into eating a poisoned apple, putting her into a deep sleep. Luckily, a prince comes riding along on a white horse and wakes her up with a kiss. Then everything turns out great. End of movie. But that queen scared me so much, I wouldn't touch an apple for months afterward.

I couldn't blame Dad for not wanting to read any books. He had to read a whole bunch of engineering books to get through college. So he was tired of reading. Besides, it made him available to play Monopoly on evenings when there weren't any good radio shows.

When Monopoly came out, it was like—wow! —this is a million times better than any board game yet. First, it involved money. Money used to buy property and houses and collect rent from the others. That was the fun of it—making money and enriching yourself at others' expense, just like real life. If you owned all of one color, you could buy houses and collect rent from anyone landing on your property.

I went for the low-rent districts, the purple Baltic-Mediterranean and the light-blue Oriental-Vermont-Connecticut. Let others work on the upper-crust Park Place and Boardwalk. I liked being a slum landlord and it paid off very well. The Waterworks and Electric Company were good, too.

"You'd make a good entrepreneur," Dad said once, handing over the last of his cash.

What's that mean?

He sounded it out. "Onta-pra-newer. It's French, I think. It means a creative businessman. Someone who takes high risks with new ideas and makes lots of money in business." That sounded great! Oh, to be an onta-pra-newer and make tons of money! Then I could be a real Lamont Cranston and be a real man-about-town in a big city like Portland!

One Saturday, Dad took us across the Columbia River for a joy-ride in Washington. There were no bridges, so we had to cross by ferry. At the waterfront, there was a paved ramp leading down to the landing. The ferry was gone, crossing the river, so all we could see was the ramp going right down into the water. For kicks, Dad came roaring down the ramp and skidded to a stop just before hitting the water. I yelled and Mom sucked in her breath. Real smart. What if the brakes had given out? I think it gave Dad some kind of sick thrill to scare us like that. Around the house, Mom called the shots. So maybe this was his way of getting even.

The so-called ferry was a little barge, only big enough to hold four cars, loosely tied to a tugboat which maneuvered the barge up to the landing. Before it could drift away, some guys chained it to a piling and pushed a wooden wedge up for cars to drive on the barge. Dad gunned the motor, drove up and aboard and set the brakes bard. Boy, was I glad to see that—I didn't want us rolling off into that deep water! After loading up another car, the tugboat pulled the barge away from shore. Then it turned and came around from behind and began pushing us across the mile-wide Columbia River. We plowed our way through white-capped waves, water splashing over the deck. When we got to the Washington side, the tugboat maneuvered around again and pushed our barge up to the ramp. Guys on that side chained the barge to a piling and pushed a wooden wedge up for the cars.

We drove off the barge and up the ramp to a paved road. Whew! Back on dry land again. We followed the road to the top, then turned right and headed east on Highway 14. Driving along, we got passed by a couple of cars with Washington plates.

"Look at those crazy Washington drivers," Dad said.

Yeah, almost crazy enough to race down a ferry ramp.

We came around a curve and saw a huge three-story building sitting on a high plateau overlooking the river.

"There's Maryhill," said Dad. "Some call it Maryhill Castle." We turned off the highway and followed a paved road toward the castle into an oasis of grass and trees. We pulled over and parked.

"This place was built by Sam Hill," said Dad. "He died a few years back, so all work has stopped inside the building. He was a railroad man, but he believed in highways. He sold the politicians on building the Columbia Gorge Highway."

Maryhill Castle looked impressive, like an old French chateau. Oh, the joy of making tons of money and having a show-off mansion—rewards for being an onta-pra-newer! Sam Hill had friends in high places, Dad said, and got Queen Marie of Romania to dedicate Maryhill back in 1926. Many people thought Hill wanted the Queen to stay and live there. But she went back to Romania. She preferred a more civilized place, I guess, like Transylvania.

After looking over Maryhill, Dad drove us a couple miles east to another grassy bluff overlooking the river. We left the highway on a gravel road and pulled up by some odd piles of concrete. "This is Stonehenge," said Dad. "It's an exact replica of the original shrine in England. It was built by Sam Hill as a war memorial in the twenties."

The place was really weird. Concrete pillars stood upright and were connected along the tops with horizontal concrete slabs to form a perfect circle. There was an altar stone in the middle and other concrete pillars here and there. It was a perfect place to hide from Skipper, then jump out and scare the crap out of him.

Leaving Stonehenge, Dad drove down the hill to another ferry landing. We went down the ramp, slow this time, and drove up on the barge. Once again, the tugboat pulled us away, then came around and pushed us across the river to a landing on the other side. Then we drove off the barge. Man, was I happy to get back to Oregon and onto dry land again!

~ * ~

We drove west on Highway 30, back toward The Dalles, along the Columbia River. Then Dad slowed down and pulled off the highway. We bumped along a narrow dirt road past other cars parked in the grass between large black rocks. We stopped and got out and walked toward a little hill where people were standing and staring out at the river. Dad led us up a trail to the top. When we got up there, we could see what they were watching. It was Indians standing on rickety platforms, holding nets in the water. Here the river dropped about twenty feet in a horseshoe falls facing the Oregon side. The black rocks extended across the river, a natural dam with many channels and waterfalls spilling over the top. We watched as they pushed their long-handled nets into the roaring waters. Sometimes a salmon would fly out of a waterfall, trying to jump the falls. Now and then an Indian would haul up a net with a huge salmon flopping like crazy.

"This is Celilo Falls," said Dad. "The Indians have been coming here to catch salmon for ten thousand years."

I felt a gentle nudge on my back. I turned around and saw—the Mexican! Holy crap! I jumped back and wanted to yell, but he put a finger to his lips and I kept quiet. He handed me a card. Then he turned and scuttled off down the hill. I turned the card over. It was a playing card. Ten of spades. Who was this guy? What did he want? And what did this playing card mean? I shivered a little and stuck it in my pocket. I looked back at the fishermen, but all I could think about was that Mexican.

Three

I carried that ten of spades in my pocket every day, looking at it all the time. What did it mean? How did that Mexican guy know where I lived? It almost drove me crazy. All I could do was carry that card, looking at it over and over. As if it had any answers. What did it mean? Why was that Mexican guy following me everywhere?

When school let out after the second grade, Dad announced we were moving back to Redmond where they had lived before. "Orders from Salem," he said, meaning the State Highway Department. It was a fantastic break. Now I could get rid of that Mexican guy! Redmond was over a hundred miles away—he could never find me there.

By then, Skipper had developed into a perfect pain-in-the-ass. He was always looking for some sneaky way of getting even, to pay me back for my kidding around with him. Mom accused me of "bullying," even though I was always good-natured about it. Just shows how the best intentions can be misunderstood. I figured he might use this move to bring down a big disaster on me. Like throwing out my bugs. I had a fantastic bug collection.

I kept all my bugs in a glass Mason jar—a yellow jacket, a moth, a beetle, a butterfly, a grasshopper, an earwig, a hornet, and a ladybug—all dead because I forgot to punch air holes in the lid. But they were a great treasure to me and I was worried about a sneak attack by that little Skipper.

During the week, Mom, Evelyn and Veronica got the dishes and all the other stuff packed up in cardboard boxes and ready to go. That week I kept my bugs with me all the time and under my pillow at night just to keep them safe from Skipper.

Then one day the moving van showed up. Two guys came in with their hand-trucks. They loaded the piano, refrigerator, sofa, easy chairs, mattresses, box springs, and dining room table and then carried the cardboard boxes to the van and shoved them in the spaces between the heavy stuff. I put my bug collection in a cardboard box just before they closed the big doors.

After they left, I climbed in the Studebaker with the others. As we rolled down Elm Street, I looked back at our big old white house for the last time. We drove east on Highway 30 along the Columbia River to Biggs Junction, then headed south on Highway 97. We drove past endless wheat fields and through little towns—Wasco, Moro and Grass Valley—and across a desert of sagebrush, lava rock and bunch grass.

As we went further south, I felt almost giddy about getting away from that Mexican. I felt like I was going deeper and deeper into a perfect hideaway, like a big old cave or some deep woods where no one knew where I was. The further we got away from The Dalles, I figured, the further I got away from the threat he posed. I wondered what he wanted to do with me. Was he gonna kidnap me and hold me for ransom? I didn't think Dad made enough money for any big ransom pay-off, so he'd be outta luck on that score. Maybe he wanted to take me someplace where he could hold me captive and turn me into a pickpocket. Or maybe he wanted to catch me and kill me just for fun. Then he could cut off my head, shrink it down and put it in a bottle for showing off to his friends in some Mexican beer joint.

We kept going further and further south, further and further into the back country where he could never find me. All those stupid thoughts, all those stupid worries about the Mexican. It would be easy to forget them once we got to Redmond, deep in the middle of nowhere. I could just imagine how pissed-off he would be when he found out I had given him the slip forever!

Dad continued driving south past Shaniko, down through Cow Canyon and into a wide bottomland of green fields and grazing cattle. We climbed again into a high range of sagebrush and juniper trees and followed the highway to a little town called Madras. We drove the one-block main street, followed the highway's sharp turn right, headed further south and drove through other little towns called Metolius and Culver. We continued south, crossed the deep canyon of the Crooked River and then finally arrived at the town of Redmond.

This town was a lot smaller than The Dalles. It was a higher elevation, too, part of the "high desert" of eastern Oregon but surrounded by irrigated potato fields and pastures, which kept the desert away. The views were fantastic, with hills and buttes on all sides. Smith Rock and Gray Butte rose up north and east of town. On the western horizon the snow-capped Cascades—Mount Hood, Mount Jefferson, Three-Fingered Jack, Mount Washington, North Sister, Middle Sister, South Sister, Broken Top, and Mount Bachelor—marched north to south along a skyline of timbered foothills.

We turned off the main street, followed a street lined with trees and lawns, turned left and pulled up in front of a house. This was our new home. Skipper and I got out to take a look. It was small, much smaller than our house in The Dalles. It didn't even have a porch. You walked up a couple of concrete steps, opened the front door and went inside. Dad had come down a few weeks earlier and bought the place. It was okay, I guess. But the best part was, I knew that Mexican guy could never find me way down here in central Oregon.

Redmond was a town of maybe eighteen hundred, with a central area about eight blocks long. Going south from town along the highway was a canal full of water flowing in from the Deschutes River. Out of that main canal came irrigation ditches running through town. One of those came through our neighborhood, just beyond the back alley. It ran as an open stream for a couple blocks, then disappeared into an underground tunnel. Once we talked about where it came out. There was some talk about getting a rubber raft and riding it underground to the next opening. Good thing we never tried it. Sometimes we watched tadpoles in the water. We heard that tadpoles turned into frogs. We wanted to watch that, but nobody would hang around long enough to see it happen. I caught a tadpole once and put it in a jar. But it died before turning into a frog. Or maybe Skipper killed it.

One day, I saw Mom measuring the outside of our house and drawing up plans on a poster board. I found out what she was up to the next Friday night after we finished off a big chicken dinner. While we were all just sitting there, she got her poster board from a closet and showed it to Dad.

"Douglas," she said, "we need to add another bedroom."

Dad shook his head. "We just bought this place. I know the house is small. But give it some time. You'll get used to it."

Mom wasn't giving any ground. "We're all cooped up in this tiny house. We need another bedroom."

Dad just sat there. He didn't say a word. He was whipped and he knew it. Mom always got the last word, especially on a big deal like this.

What he did next was typical. He got up suddenly, grabbed a cigar, jammed on his hat, and left for a long walk. Looking out the window, I could see him charging down the sidewalk. Mom just went back to clearing plates off the table, serene in the knowledge that she had won again.

A couple hours later, Dad came walking back in the darkness. Mom had gone to bed by then. He came inside, plunked his hat on the rack, snuffed out his cigar, and went in the kitchen. I sneaked over to watch as he stood before the kitchen cabinet. He reached up above the cabinet, pulled down a bottle of wine and popped the cork. He tipped the bottle back and took a long swig. He pushed the cork in and carefully laid the bottle on top of the cabinet, out of sight. Then he went back into the living room, sat and listened to some news on the radio and shuffled off to bed.

~ * ~

There was a red-headed girl living next door, built pretty solid and looking about a year older than me. I watched her riding her bike up and down the street. I got jealous as hell 'cause I didn't have a bike and I couldn't ride one anyway. One day, she came coasting up to our front lawn and stopped where I was standing.

"I see you moved in the other day," she said. "I'm Jennifer. Jennifer Erickson. What's your name?"

"Hamilton Skutt."

"Hamilton Skutt," she repeated. "That's a tough one. I'll just call you Ham-Bone. You okay with that?"

I nodded and she took off. Now I wanted a bike more than ever. I pestered Mom over and over until she finally gave up and bought me a used bike. Only problem was, I didn't know how to ride it. Finally, I decided to hell with it. I decided to just take a chance and try it.

Old Jennifer gave me a shove to get me started. I was scared I would fall over, but somehow, I didn't. As long as I kept that bike moving, I didn't fall over. Fantastic! After a few more shoves by Jennifer, I learned how to push the bike, get it rolling and then jump on. Now I didn't need any help from anybody. Now I could ride that bike wherever I wanted to go. Each day, I jumped on the bike and rode it up and down the street. I just couldn't believe how easy it was to go places, even all the way downtown.

One day, Mom decided to take me to see Doc Jenkins. For a checkup, I guess. She left Skipper with Veronica and we took off. We walked four blocks and came to a one-story concrete building. This was the doctor's office. We walked in and the woman at the desk said he could see us right away. She led us down a hallway and into a little room.

We sat there a few minutes. Then the door swung open and in came a huge guy, maybe three hundred pounds, with a red face of six chins and a toothy smile. He wore a gray suit with white shirt and tie. He looked more like a car salesman than a doctor. Mom said when

I was born here in Redmond seven years earlier, he was the doctor. When I heard that, I sucked in my breath, figuring I had dodged a bullet.

"Hello, Doctor," said Mom. "This is my son, Hamilton. You've met before, I think."

"You bet we've met before!" boomed the doctor. He put on that big grin again, leaned way down and got right in my face. "Son!" he boomed, with a kind of expectant look on his face, "I brought you into the world!" Then he got busy. He took my blood pressure, listened to my chest and told me to take deep breaths—the usual doctor moves while deciding how much to charge, and then he quit all that and put his stuff away. "You're sound as a dollar, my boy!" he boomed again, with that grinning look of great expectations. What did he want, for God's sake, a tip?

With the exam over, they got to talking about that great day when I was born. It had happened in a little house they rented down on the north end of town, on a cold December day in the late twenties. Mom had to postpone some plans to get installed in the P.E.O. Club. She finally made it okay. She wasn't initiated or inducted. She was installed, like putting a new sink in the bathroom.

"Well, Doctor Jenkins, I just wanted you to see Hamilton, so you could see how much he has grown." The doctor smiled, nodded and jiggled his six chins. On the walk downtown, Mom had said the doctor sometimes got paid by the farmers with sacks of potatoes and sides of beef. I could see the good doctor had found his proper calling and enjoyed all the rewards of his medical practice. It looked like he hadn't missed any meals or ever been late getting to the table.

Before going back home, Mom said she had to stop by a lawyer's office to sign some papers about the house. We climbed some stairs to a second-story office over a clothing store. We went in the office door, marked in big fancy letters:

Lowell Savage, Attorney-at-Law.

I kinda shivered, going into that big fancy office with thick rugs, dark wood paneling and polished conference tables. But Mom wasn't bothered one little bit. She walked up to the receptionist and asked to see Mr. Savage. Before we could sit down, a little short guy came out of another office and scurried over.

"Mrs. Skutt, I believe?" Mom nodded. "We have some papers for you to sign on your new home. Your husband signed them on a previous trip to Redmond."

This was all boring stuff, but the lawyer caught my interest. He had a permanent frown like he had just bitten into some juniper berries. But he also had a crafty look, like a kid plotting to steal a candy bar out of your lunch box. He was trying to be nice and friendly, even trying to force a smile while Mom was signing the papers. But all he could do was get his face so twisted and contorted it looked like he was having a big silent scream. Mom finally finished signing the papers and handed them back.

He took the papers with an air of receiving the Holy Grail. He held them with both hands, like holding a baby, and gingerly carried them to the receptionist. She took them with a similar reverence, having been well schooled by Mr. Attorney-at-Law.

Mom and the lawyer said the usual thank-yous and goodbyes and we left. On the way back, we walked past Mr. Savage's house. Mom pointed it out to me. It was a huge white palace sitting on a half-block of manicured lawns and shrubbery and surrounded by a high chain-link fence. To keep out those he had ruined, no doubt.

Not long after I was born came Black Tuesday, Oct. 29, 1929, when the stock market crashed. On Wall Street, they said, stockbrokers and clients were jumping out of skyscrapers. Back in Redmond, I don't think it made much of a ripple. Probably nobody in town owned any stocks anyway, except maybe a few people like Doc Jenkins and Mr. Savage.

I doubt if either one of them tried to jump off a roof there in town. The only place high enough was the Odd Fellows Hall or the Redmond Hotel. The hotel had awnings over the front sidewalk which would spoil a fall. If they'd tried the back-alley side, all they would've done was maybe break a leg when they bounced off the garbage cans.

One Saturday morning, Dad said he was going downtown to get a haircut. He asked if I wanted to come along and get a haircut, too. Of course, I said yes. Mom had always cut my hair before. But now I was going to get it cut by a real barber, just like the big guys.

We walked downtown, Dad puffing on a cigar and strolling along in an easy gait as I ran to keep up. We took a left turn and walked down the sidewalk past a drug store and a hardware store. We came to a place with an upright cylinder outside, red and white stripes turning slowly—the barbershop. Dad opened the door and we went inside.

The place reeked with the smell of lotions, and hummed with the sound of clippers clipping and the buzz of many voices. Bits of hair littered the floor, now and then swept up by a barber into a pile at the corner. Huge mirrors filled the back wall. Lined up along the other walls were chairs full of men waiting their turn. They were having a good time, I could tell, and nobody was in a big hurry to get finished and leave.

There were two guys in bib overalls and muddy boots, maybe some potato growers or dairy farmers. One guy was dressed in a suit... an insurance guy or maybe just a banker. Another man wore slacks and plaid shirt...a teacher or a merchant. Another had ragged jeans, cut off at the shins...a logger or just a worker from the pine mill. They were talking about hog prices and football and more irrigation water coming in.

"Looks like the city council is gonna raise taxes for paving more streets," said the guy in the suit.

"Over my dead body," said the guy in the plaid shirt. Everybody kinda snickered and went back to talking.

"Didya hear 'bout the county commissioner?" asked the guy in ragged jeans. "Didya hear what happin' to 'im over in Bend?"

"You mean ol' man Morrison?" said the guy in the plaid shirt. "Yeah, I heard he had a stroke."

"Yeah! In a cathouse!" said the guy in ragged jeans. "The girl he had just about went crazy!"

Everybody broke out laughing. Some were laughing so hard they choked and coughed and finished up wiping tears from their eyes. The guy in the suit tried to shush the guy in jeans. He put a finger to his mouth and pointed at me.

"What, the kid?" asked the guy in ragged jeans. "Don't worry. He don't know what the hell a cathouse is anyhow!"

He was right. I didn't know what the hell a cathouse was. But I sure wanted to find out. I looked at Dad. He was pretending to read an old *Look* magazine, but he had a tiny smile on his face.

"Which cathouse was it?" asked one of the guys in bib overalls.

"The Cozy Rooms, I think," answered the guy in ragged jeans. This got them laughing all over again.

What was it all about? It didn't make any sense. I knew a stroke was bad news. So why were they laughing? What's so funny about having a stroke in a cathouse? And what's a cathouse?

I gave up trying to figure it out. These guys seemed to be happy just sitting in this barbershop. Maybe they were happy just getting away from their jobs or wives or whatever troubles they had. I could see this was a special place for them. If their hair didn't grow out, they would've found some other reason to come in here. Maybe get their toenails trimmed.

After Dad got his haircut, it was my turn. When the barber pointed at me, I stood up and walked to the chair like I was advancing to the throne of England.

The barber got a board and set it across the arms of the chair and I climbed up on it. As I sat there getting clipped, I felt really proud to be old enough to come to the barbershop. I thought about growing up to my full height and sitting in the chair without a board and talking about a county commissioner getting a stroke in a cathouse. I knew that someday I would share in the joys of finding refuge in a barbershop. And I knew that someday I would find out just what the hell a cathouse was.

~ * ~

One day, a truck full of lumber pulled up in front of our house. A boss man got out, with three other guys, and came up to the front door. Mom went outside and showed them where to stack the lumber in the back yard. With her drawing, she showed them the new bedroom dimensions and where to build it. The boss man had them run a tape measure over the grass, stake the corners and pull the strings tight to show the exact lines where the walls were supposed to go. The new bedroom project was underway.

It took several weeks from start to finish. On the first day, the crew dug trenches along the string lines to outline the bedroom. I watched all this, fascinated by their easy confidence. When I talked with the guys during lunch breaks, they seemed to get a kick out of explaining things. The boss man wasn't so friendly. He was an old grouch with a moustache, a goatee and narrow eyes.

During the construction, I kept my eyes on the boss man. In fact, I watched his every move. I watched how he ordered the men around, watched him get right down in there with the workers when they needed an extra guy to help out. I wondered about him. I wondered, is he the real ontapra-newer of this outfit or just a straw boss getting paid a little extra to run the operation? If he was the owner, I wondered how much money he would make off this job. If he was the owner, maybe he had to borrow money to buy all the lumber, cement, and other stuff and pay the other guys. After the job was all done, he'd have to pay off all the loans and hope there was some money left over for him. I wondered how many construction jobs this crew did in a year. If they did, say, eight jobs a year, it could add up to something pretty good. What if something went wrong? What if the homeowner lost his job and couldn't pay? What would the boss man do then? Knock the guy down and stomp him silly?

In the trenches, they placed iron rods, or rebar, and fixed forms for piers lined up on the ground to support the floor. When the concrete truck showed up, they poured wet cement into the trenches and forms to make the piers and foundation walls around the whole bedroom.

Next, they built a platform across the foundation walls. They laid down heavy upright lumber supported by the piers. Over that they nailed a sub-floor of planks in a diagonal pattern. Over the sub-floor they finished the floor with a covering of smooth thick plywood. So far, so good.

Then they used the new floor as a platform to frame the wall sections. As each wall was completed, with holes for windows, they raised it and kept it upright with temporary supports. The walls looked so flimsy standing there, just two-by-fours nailed together, I couldn't believe they could hold up the whole roof. But that's what happened. After a truck came with pre-built wooden triangles, or trusses, they were hoisted up above the walls and nailed into place.

They built the roof by nailing lumber to connect the trusses and built the ceiling inside the room. They nailed exterior plywood, or sheathing, to the walls and roof and stapled tarpaper over that. They tacked on asphalt shingles to the roof and laid insulation in the attic. Then they put the windows in and nailed on horizontal siding to match the rest of the house. In the new bedroom, they ran electric cables through the studs, installed an electric heater and stuffed insulation between the studs. Then they nailed slabs of sheetrock inside and plastered on the finish.

Toward the end of the project, I walked up to the boss-man one day.

"Are you an "onta-pra-newer?"

"Whoa! Where'd you get a big word like that, kid?"

"From Dad. He told me ont-pra-newers are businessmen who make tons of money."

"Well, I'm not an onta-screw-it." I'm a builder. I bid on a job, buy the materials, hire the men and work with them to finish the job. When all the bills are paid, maybe I'll have some left for myself. Maybe not."

"You must have some kind of cushion—"

"Cushion, bullshit. There's always something to screw up the works. Like you talking with the men."

"But I—"

"Look, kid, let's face it. With you nosing around here, asking questions, taking up my men's time, you're costing me money. You're a pain-in-the-ass. I don't want you hanging around here anymore. Got that?"

I nodded and walked away. What a phony bastard! Seems like all the grownups are phony bastards. Maybe the kids should take over running the world and let the grownups stay home with their dolls and toy trucks. But wait. The kids would be lousy businessmen. They would just give everything away. Before you knew it, everybody would be broke. Guess the grownups need to keep it after all.

Across the street from our house was a high brick wall which ran around the whole block. We could see tops of trees inside the grounds, but nothing else. On the other side of the block was a paved driveway with a black wrought-iron gate closed off to us local yokels. We could look in just far enough to see the driveway curving off into the trees. Everybody was so curious about this place. Inside those brick walls, it was said, was a lush landscape like the Hanging Gardens of Babylon. In the midst of all that splendor was a castle from the Arabian Nights, a palace of crystal chandeliers and shining marble floors covered with exotic oriental rugs. I could imagine it all, another trophy mansion by another successful onta-pra-newer. It made me kinda jealous, to tell the truth. Jennifer had heard all about this walled paradise from some kid who really had the scoop on it. And now she wanted more.

"What we need," she said, "is somebody with enough guts to climb the wall." She gave me a look that I recognized right off.

"Oh, no! Not me! Get somebody else!"

"So you're chicken—is that it?"

She had me there. I was trapped.

"Got a ladder?"

"You bet!" she yelled and ran back to her garage. There was no way out. I was whipped. She came out, dragging a long wooden ladder. She leaned the ladder up against the brick wall. It was just the right length, about a foot higher than the wall.

With a sinking heart, I started climbing up the ladder. I stepped on the first rung, stood for a minute, took the next rung, stood for a minute, stepped on another rung and stood for a minute. Even with my stalling, I was up there before I knew it, looking over the wall.

"What do you see, Ham-Bone?" yelled Jennifer.

"Nothin' yet. I can't see nothin' but grass and trees."

"Then climb up over and jump down inside," she yelled.

I was trapped. Absolutely trapped. There was no way out. I had no choice but to climb up over the wall and jump—

"Dinner's ready!" came Mom's voice from our front door across the street. Boy, was I happy to hear that!

"I'm coming!" I yelled as I flew down the ladder. "Gotta go for dinner," I yelled at old Jennifer as I ran back across the street.

The next day, she tried to coax me up the ladder again. But it didn't work anymore, all that talk about me being chicken, and she finally gave up. We just stopped worrying about what was behind that stupid brick wall. It was a good thing, too. They probably had some Dobermans running around those palatial grounds just waiting for a tasty meal like me.

~ * ~

One Saturday, Dad drove us to Bend, a big town about sixteen miles away. Going south, we followed the highway over a landscape of sagebrush and juniper trees—desert land, not yet irrigated for some reason—which turned green again with pastures and hayfields along both sides of the highway as we got closer to town.

Bend outclassed Redmond in every way possible. For starters, it was a big city of eight thousand people. And loaded with trees. Not ugly junipers or even cottonwoods, but Ponderosa pines standing tall around town and gracing a big grassy park along the Deschutes River, Good old Redmond would never win a beauty contest with Bend, that's for sure.

Still, Redmond was a great place for kids in the summertime. No school, of course, and the climate was perfect with dry air and sunshine. At noon each day, the stupid city fire alarm sounded. Otherwise, it was quiet. A dog might bark. Then it got quiet again. Sometimes, though, a sound came along that grabbed you by the throat.

This sound came without warning. One day in mid-summer, I heard it for the first time. It was a bugle call at five o'clock in the morning. Dad said it was "reveille"—the Army's wake-up call—and it came from a C.C.C. camp set up just outside of town. That was the Civilian Conservation Corps.

Dad said the Depression put people out of work, and the government set up this program to create jobs for city boys working in the woods. I wasn't too sure what a Depression was. But I knew from the newsreels it was bad news Back East, with guys in soup lines and other guys selling apples on the street. It was depressing all right. I was glad that stuff wasn't happening here. I felt sorta guilty that we had dodged it somehow. Then I thought about the Mexican. How come *he* didn't have to work? How come he had the time to chase me down and give me that ten of spades? And what did the card mean? Was he going to stab me or something? Was he getting some kind of sick thrill scaring me like this and making me sweat little green apples until the day he showed up to finish me off?

Before I knew it, summer had slipped away and it was time to go back to school. This grade school was new for me, but that was okay. I was a seasoned third-grader, familiar with all the customs of grade school life. Getting there was a cinch. All I had to do was walk a block toward downtown, turn left, cross the street, walk another two blocks past the high school and cross that street to reach the school.

Redmond Grade School was a one-story brick building on a half-block of grass and playground. Our teacher, I found out, was an old guy with a patch of white hair, white eyebrows, half-moon glasses and deep wrinkles around his mouth. His hands shook sometimes and he walked bent over like he was looking for something. That was Mr. Philpott. He had been there forever, it was said, and they couldn't get him to retire. Sometimes he stuck his finger in his ear and pulled it out and took a long look at whatever came out. What did he expect to find except earwax?

For an old guy, though, he had a great throwing arm. Once he was upfront erasing the blackboard, Rich Daniels and I were clowning around in the back of the room. We had just come in from recess and had a contest going, making fart noises by blowing on our arms and laughing our heads off.

All of a sudden, Mr. Philpott whirled around, fired his eraser and hit me right on the head—BAM! What a shot! Both Daniels and I shut up right away and headed straight back to our stupid desks.

Mr. Philpott had many tricks up his sleeve. Once he put me in "prison" under an empty desk on the front row. That was okay with me. I'd been flirting with Kathy Allen, who sat right behind my jail. In my solitary confinement, I was able to tap out a message to her on the wood panel between us. She even tapped out a reply with her shoe. Now encouraged, I reached under the panel and touched her ankle. Somehow it gave me a big thrill. That old tingling sensation again. It was even better 'cause she didn't pull her foot away like I expected.

Another time, Mr. Philpott caught me acting crazy in the back of the room and told me to come up front. When I got there, he asked me if I was a good athlete. Of course, I nodded. He gave me some chalk, told me to reach up as high as I could, and make a mark on the blackboard. Eager to show off my athletic ability, I stretched just as high as I could and made a mark.

"Okay, good," he said. "Now hold the chalk on that mark until I tell you to quit."

I stayed up there on tip-toes, stretching hard as I could to keep the chalk on the mark. I stood there, shaking and sweating for an eternity, desperately straining to hold the chalk on the line. "Okay, you can quit now," he said, and I dropped like a limp rag. Walking back to my desk, I had to admit that old Mr. Philpott had the last laugh that time.

Somehow, Mom got the idea that I could be a great violinist, maybe the next Jascha Heifetz. So she signed me up for violin lessons with a nice old lady from church. I didn't mind going for the lessons each week. With the violin case in my bicycle basket, I rode downtown to the Odd Fellows Hall. In a dusty little room upstairs, I learned how to push the bow over the strings while holding my left-hand fingers in different ways to screech out the so-called music. The time went by pretty fast, and then I was free to go. What I hated, though, was her orders to practice an hour each day. That was tough to take—an hour each day of practice on that stupid violin.

Then one day I got an inspiration. I waited until Dad got home from work before starting practice. He usually sat in his easy chair, looking at a *Life* magazine while waiting for dinner. Sawing away in my bedroom, I heard him moving around the house, kinda restless-like. I heard him go outside, trying in vain to escape the sound. I kept up this way of practicing for a couple of weeks until it finally paid off.

One morning after breakfast, Mom looked at me with an expression of compassion, or even pity. "Don't go just yet," she said. "There's something I need to tell you."

I sat back down at the table.

She looked at me like she had really bad news. "Your father thinks you should give up the violin lessons," she said with obvious pain. "Maybe you could try another musical instrument." She hesitated again, as if trying to shield me from the next blow. "Say, in four or five years."

I stood and gave a little sigh. "Okay," I said. "Whatever Dad wants is fine with me. I have to leave for school now." With a sad expression, I walked out the front door and headed for school. It was all I could do to keep from pumping my fists and jumping for joy.

For months afterward, Mom told her friends how proud she was that her son could handle adversity with such fortitude and backbone.

Four

Mom and Dad had a good social life in Redmond. Dad joined the Free Masons, the biggest lodge in town. Once a week, he went down to the Masonic Lodge dressed up in his best suit. The town butcher always wore a shiny black suit with starched white shirt and red tie. They called him Worshipful Master, so you can see why he liked it. Mom was already a fixture in the P.E.O. Club and then she joined the Order of the Eastern Star.

They also belonged to a private bridge club which met every Saturday night at somebody's house. Sometimes the club came to our house. Dad carefully wrote down all the scores every week and kept those records for years. He and Mom talked about bridge all the time. They bought books on how to play like experts. They studied those books over and over and tried to make all the great strategies work. But it didn't seem to help much. Dad, especially, always griped about his lousy scores.

"I could be a great bridge player," he said, "if only somebody would deal me some decent cards."

You can have my ten of spades, I thought. A ten of spades that probably means a whole lot more than some stupid bridge game.

Sometimes I came home from school and found a bunch of ladies in our house. That was Mom's afternoon bridge club, which met every other week at somebody's place. They seemed to have a lot more fun than the Saturday night bunch. They looked a lot happier and more relaxed. For one thing, nobody seemed to care much about the score or who won the game.

And nobody got all steamed up keeping all those stupid records. What they really cared about was eating.

Those ladies looked pretty well fed. Mom was kind of plump, but she looked downright scrawny compared with those others. I never saw them play much bridge, come to think of it. They hung around the kitchen, just gossiping and waiting for the coffee and dessert. Once I went in the kitchen and I was bowled over by the wonderful smell of coffee percolating. I hadn't even tasted coffee yet, but the smell was delicious.

Other good smells came from the bananas, pineapple and other stuff on top of the cakes and pies, smothered with mounds of whipped cream. With the coffee smells and piles of sweet desserts and good friends wolfing it down, our house seemed like the happiest place on earth.

Whenever we could beg a couple dimes off Mom, Skipper and I walked downtown to take in a movie. Most of them were black-and-white Westerns starring Hopalong Cassidy or Gene Autry. In the movies, the good guys wore white hats and the bad guys wore black ones. It helped keep track of who to cheer for. Sometimes Gene Autry rode into town, went into a saloon for coffee and got in a fight with the bad guys. Sometimes he helped the down-trodden sheepherders fight off the crooked cattlemen. And sometimes he chased the bad guys after they had robbed the bank.

No matter what started it, Gene Autry and his pals always ended up racing their horses through the same country full of rocks. Not black and jagged ones. These movie rocks were white, smooth and big as cars. If you watched the bad guys and good guys long enough, you saw them racing past the same rocks they had galloped past earlier.

What were they doing, going around in circles? At the end of each movie, Gene Autry got out his guitar and sang "Back in the Saddle Again." I began to wonder about this guy. Where was the guitar when he was chasing the bad guys? How come he always hugged his horse instead of the girl? Why was I even watching this stuff?

Maybe the theater owner had the same questions, 'cause he started bringing in better movies. Like a good onta-pra-newer, his promotion scheme was fantastic. Each month, he sent out a calendar showing the span of each movie over the days it was playing. Big, exciting scenes spread over three or four days. Each month, that calendar made you ache to see each new movie. And the theater was almost always filled up, thanks to his great promotion idea.

Then Clark Gable movies started popping up like popcorn. One was *Call of The Wild* with Gable and his buddy Jack Oakie set during the Klondike gold rush. Gable has a dog named Buck he bought for his lead sled dog. Heading north, they rescue Loretta Young from some wolves. Her husband has disappeared, apparently dragged off by the wolves, so they take her along to Dawson City. After a brief stay, Gable and Oakie and Young leave for the Klondike and find an old shack along a stream. Gable turns the shack into a cozy cabin and soon they are piling up bags full of gold dust. Oakie goes back to Dawson, leaving Gable alone with Young. Then some crooks come along and rob their gold. And Young's husband shows up. He takes her away in a canoe and Buck runs off to join a wolf pack. Gable ends up like a sap, doing all the work only to lose his gold and girlfriend and dog.

Another movie was *Mutiny on the Bounty*. This one had Gable as first officer on the *HMS Bounty*, sent from England to gather breadfruit plants from Tahiti. Charles Laughton is Captain Bligh, a sadistic tyrant who has the men flogged for no good reason. Tahiti is a paradise for the men, who spend all their time on shore with the sexy native girls. When the ship leaves, the men stage a mutiny and Gable is their leader. They put Laughton and his die hard supporters adrift in a small boat. They sail back to Tahiti to pick up their girlfriends and manage to reach Pitcairn Island. When Gable and his gang set fire to the *Bounty*, you knew they were stuck on that cruddy island forever.

Still another movie was *San Francisco*, with Clark Gable as the owner of a Barbary Coast saloon around 1906. Into this sleazy joint one day comes Jeanette MacDonald, who gets hired as a singer by Gable. His best pal is Spencer Tracy, a priest, who says Gable is off-base trying to make out with MacDonald. I had to agree with Tracy. She looked way too innocent for Gable. She really belonged with Nelson Eddy, a Canadian Mounty with a Smokey Bear hat, in another movie. One time, MacDonald is singing in Gable's joint. Some guy from Nob Hill hears her sing and gets her a job singing with the opera. This upsets Gable and he tries to force her back into the saloon job. All this is just shadow-boxing before the big event. It happens right on schedule—the Big Earthquake of 1906.

All these little troubles don't amount to anything as the ground shakes and buildings collapse and fires break out all over the city. Gable rushes into the street, dodging falling walls as people scream and horses gallop by pulling fire pumps. He staggers all over the burning city looking for MacDonald. After a long search, he finds her in a big park with thousands of other people singing hymns as the city burns in the background. Gable grabs MacDonald and vows to change his evil ways. Not sure how that worked out, but I figured he had to close down his Barbary Coast joint and let her keep singing for the opera.

Each afternoon after school, I came home, turned on the floor-model Philco radio and rolled the tuner over the yellow dial to find the right station for the program I wanted. As I stared into the speakers, I imagined all the action going along with the sounds. Depending on the day of the week, I listened to the roaring engine of Captain Midnight's plane or the Comanche war cry of Straight Arrow or music announcing the arrival of Little Orphan Annie.

On the Orphan Annie program, they offered a Magic Decoder Badge so I could decipher secret messages sent over the air and get the answers to all kinds of mysteries. They said to take the seals off two Ovaltine boxes and send them in with a dime for postage. So I pestered Mom until she finally broke down and bought me a couple cans of the stuff. I opened the cans, took out the seals and sent them off with a dime. Then I sat back and waited as the days crawled by.

One day the mailman delivered some letters and bills as usual, dropping them through a metal slot near the front door. I found the pile and noticed a flat little package with my name on it. I tore off the wrapping paper, opened a little box and there was my Magic Decoder Badge! Now I had the power to answer any question and solve any mystery! Then I spotted something else in the pile—a white envelope with my name and address printed in big letters. I got a kitchen knife and slashed it open. I reached in and pulled something out. It was the jack of spades.

Holy crap—that damned Mexican! How did he find me here in Redmond, a hundred miles from The Dalles? How did he know my name? And my address? What was he gonna do next? Maybe grab me on the way to school? I went into a panic. I didn't know what to do. I couldn't think of any way to get away from him. All I could do was stare at that jack of spades. First a ten of spades. Now a jack of spades. What did they mean? My Magic Decoder Badge wasn't any help, so I threw it away. Stupid piece of junk!

Then school closed for the summer. At least I didn't have to worry about getting grabbed on the way. And I could say goodbye to old Mr. Philpott and his devious tricks to get the upper hand on me. Still, I kinda wished I had talked with the clever old bastard. Maybe he could've given me some clues about that Mexican sonofabitch and his cards. Maybe he could've figured out what it was all about.

One day, Dad said he was going to buy a boat and take up lake fishing in central Oregon. He checked the ads for several days, called people on the phone and sometimes drove over to see them. Then, one Saturday morning, he took off and came back pulling a trailer holding a rowboat with an outboard motor. He was standing next to it in the driveway, grinning like crazy.

"Here she is!" he said. "We'll take her out next weekend!"

During the week, Dad made several visits to the hardware store. He came back with fishing poles, reels, lures, spinners, leaders, and other fishing stuff. And he brought back some inside dope. "No use trying to fish at Suttle Lake," he said. "They talked me out of it. Fishing's better at Elk Lake or CuItus Lake on Century Drive. But the very best place for trout fishing is East Lake. The lake is on the bottom of Newberry Crater, an old volcano near LaPine."

Next Saturday mornmg, Dad hitched his trailer-and-boat to the car and loaded up the fishing gear. It was a two-day trip, with plans for me and Dad and Evelyn to stay overnight at the lake and fish on Sunday. So we had to pack in groceries and kitchen utensils, along with sleeping bags and pillows. We finally got away in early afternoon.

We headed south, drove through Bend, past Lava Butte, and on through open pine forests. Just short of LaPine, we came to a sign pointing left to Newberry Crater. Dad turned off and we headed east along a gravel road climbing up toward the rim of the old volcano.

The old Studebaker struggled to keep going. The once-proud Dictator, sister-ship of the Dillinger getaway car, was now an exhausted beast of burden. Like Seabiscuit pulling a hay wagon. The old car, pulling the boat trailer, fought to gain elevation. As we pushed it higher and higher up the gravel road, it made strange boiling sounds and the water gauge surged into the red zone. Dad stopped, popped the hood and opened the cap as the radiator shot off clouds of steam like a volcano itself. He got some water from a little creek for the radiator. Once the car cooled off, we pulled back on the road. We made it to the rim, drove down through hillsides of black-glass obsidian and forests of lodgepole pine and arrived at East Lake.

It was a strange lake, with seaweed just offshore and the smell of sulfur from tiny bubbles in the water. Dad stopped at the main lodge office to rent a cabin. We drove over to our cabin and parked the car and trailer alongside a woodpile. We carried our stuff inside, put sleeping bags on the beds and groceries and pans in the kitchen. Evelyn worked to fix some supper while Dad and I walked along the shore to check out the lake.

When we got back, Evelyn had set the table and was frying some pork chops. We sat down and ate without much talk. Afterward, I helped Evelyn clear the table and wash dishes while Dad kept busy lighting some kerosene lamps. Before long, we crawled into our sleeping bags, blew out the lanterns and went to sleep.

Early the next morning, Dad got up, built a fire in the stove and brewed some coffee. He shook Evelyn awake and I woke up and we all stumbled into the kitchen. Evelyn fixed breakfast while Dad talked about how good the fishing would be if he could find the right spot. He said the hardware store guy told him to line up from a white slide on the north crater wall with the main lodge on the southeast shore. He described this like it was the map to a buried treasure.

Dad went out and fired up the car. He drove it down to the lake, made a big circle and backed the boat trailer into the water. He made sure all the right stuff was in the boat—the fishing poles, the tackle box, and big wiggly worms crawling around in a package filled with moss. He undid the straps holding the trailer and shoved the boat into the water. As it floated, he took the bow rope, pulled the boat back to shore and tied the rope to a big rock. Then he drove the car and trailer back to the cabin. We were almost ready to go fishing.

While Dad was launching the boat, I just stood there watching. Evelyn was back at the cabin, cleaning up from breakfast and getting all ready to go. Suddenly a little girl appeared from out of nowhere.

"Hi," she said. I looked at her. She was about my size and about my age. She had an angelic expression, with big blue eyes and a cascade of blonde curls which framed her soft lovely face.

"Hi," I replied.

"What are you doing?" she asked with an innocent smile.

"Can't you see? Going fishing with my dad and sister."

"Why don't you stay here instead? Why don't you say you're sick or something?"

"Why would I do that?"

"So you can stay here. With me. So we could go hiking."

"Why would we do that?"

"So we could go hiking over there, over in the deep woods. Out of sight of everybody. Then we could fool around." She smiled again, a kind of wicked smile this time, a smile promising pleasures beyond belief.

My heart was pounding. "What do you mean, fool around?"

She took a step forward, face-to-face now, somehow even more determined by my ignorance. "Just try it," she said, with that wicked smile. "You might like it."

By that time, Dad and Evelyn were almost back to the boat. I was in way over my head and way out of my league. "I have to go fishing with my dad and sister," I blurted out. "I can't get out of it now."

She looked at me with a kind of wonder and disbelief. Then she turned and walked away. I watched her go, longing to run after her, to tell her I didn't have to go fishing after all. To tell her we could still go hiking over in the woods. To tell her we could still fool around.

But I didn't. I just followed Dad's orders to climb in the boat with Evelyn as he shoved off from shore. Numb with remorse, I watched as he climbed aboard the stupid boat. If only she had given me some warning! If only I had time to plan something! Why didn't she come around the night before? Maybe I could've made some plans to get sick! Maybe I could've stuck my finger down my throat, maybe puked all over the place—that would've worked! Why did she wait 'til the last minute when it was too late? I got that old tingling feeling again, now mixed with heaps of self-contempt.

Dad fired up the Evinrude and we skimmed across the water, across the lake to that special spot on a sight-line from the white slide and the main lodge. He cut the motor and we drifted for a while and finally stopped. Then he grabbed the anchor and threw it in the water.

Each of us had a pole, rigged up and ready to go. We baited our hooks with the worms and cast our lines out. Then Dad opened up some cans of corn and threw the corn out in all directions. I watched the bright yellow kernels sink slowly out of sight. I thought of myself, sinking into the deep water, falling away from a golden opportunity.

We sat there for a while holding our poles. I looked back to the east rim, imagining myself with this girl up there in the woods fooling around. What would be happening right now, right at this very moment?

Suddenly Evelyn's pole dropped to the water. She screamed and yanked back hard and started reeling in like crazy. Then Dad's pole jumped and he yanked and began reeling in. Then I felt a jerk and yanked back hard to set the hook. All of us were reeling and yelling and moving the poles around, trying to keep lines untangled, Dad leaning out to net the fish.

After a couple of hours, we had caught our limit. We had a good catch.

But so what? All I could think about was that little blonde girl back on the beach. We reeled in our lines and Dad pulled the anchor and fired up the motor and we headed back. I watched the shoreline come nearer and nearer, hoping the girl was still there. As we got in close, Dad cut the motor and we glided onto the gravelly beach. I jumped out and ran along the shore, looking for her. But it was too late. She was gone. I didn't even know her name or where she lived. Worse yet, I wasn't even sure what she meant by "fooling around."

Five

Early that fall, we took a trip over to Eugene on the other side of the mountains. Other side of the Cascade mountains, volcanic peaks rising ten thousand feet perched like big saw-teeth along the western skyline. The highways threaded between the peaks, with summits around five thousand. Our highway, the McKenzie Pass, was snowbound each winter but now free of the deep snow and open for passage.

We went so Dad and Mom could visit Grandma Mueller and my sister Evelyn and watch an Oregon football game, maybe not in that order. They took Skipper and me along to keep track of us. I was happy to get out of town and not have to worry about that damned Mexican.

We drove west through Sisters and followed the highway climbing up to McKenzie Pass. At the summit, we stopped to look at the lava rock all over the place. To the north, Mt. Washington shot skyward like a Matterhorn. To the south, the North Sister glaciers loomed up thousands of feet above us.

Back in the car, we continued on past little lakes and mountain meadows along the spine of the Cascades. Then we plunged down the other side, following the loops of highway through lush rain forests, down to Belknap Springs and along the white-water rapids of the McKenzie River.

When we got to Eugene, Dad drove straight to Grandma's house. Their plan was to visit her before going to the game, but we got there too late for that. So they just dropped Skipper and me off at the curb and left us to the tender mercies of Grandma.

In the movies, grandmothers are sweet old dears with tender eyes and plump cheeks smiling with boundless love for their little grandchildren. The makers of those movies never heard of Grandma Mueller. She looked like the Wicked Old Witch in my *Hansel and Gretel* book. She always wore the same sinister black dress with evil lace around the collar. Her face looked like old leather stretched over high cheekbones, with a jutting chin and thin gray hair pulled back into a tight bun at the back of her neck. Her eyes were cold and her black eyebrows framed in a perpetual frown, her teeth sharp and pointed as though ready to take a big bite out of a poor half-assed helpless grandson.

She lived in an old two-story pioneer-style house, its square-box dimensions broken by a mid-level roof over the front porch. It was just off the university campus, oddly next door to the swanky Kappa Alpha Theta sorority house—a mecca for phony college boys driving up in convertibles to collect their lovely girls in clinging silk skirts and fur coats.

Eugene seemed like an oasis of collegiate joy. Everything was exotic and wonderful to a kid from the high desert east of the mountains. In my imagination, it was a place of moss and moisture and soft moonlit nights. The air smelled of grass, trees, roses, ivy, shrubbery, and all kinds of stuff growing in all shades of green.

This was great, but Skipper and I still had to face Grandma. As we walked up to the house, we saw a figure in black lurking behind a window of lacy curtains. We saw a gnarled old hand holding the curtains, then a glimpse of her ancient face with its menacing glare. The curtains closed with a swish and our hearts sank at the thought of going any closer. As we gingerly took the first step to the porch, the front door suddenly sprang open. We stopped, then held hands to gather up enough courage to force ourselves onward. Soon as we crossed the threshold, she slammed the door shut, like a jailer slamming a cell door.

"Hello, Grandma," I said.

"Hello, Grandma," said Skipper.

No answer. No simple "hello" to return our greetings. Certainly no hugging or kissing. That was good. I knew her gas-fired oven was on—I could smell something cooking—and I didn't want her to grab me. I didn't wanna take a chance on getting thrown into her oven. If she had grabbed Skipper, I would've kicked her in the shins until she let him go. I knew he would do the same for me.

Without a word, she jabbed a finger toward the front room and hustled off into the kitchen. We breathed a sigh of relief to be left alone. We opened a glass-fronted cabinet door and took out some board games. One of these was a horse-racing game, a steeplechase race with hazards to jump over in the race to the finish line. It was a dumb boring game, to tell the truth, but there was nothing any better. There was no Monopoly game, but that was okay. Skipper couldn't play it yet anyway. Maybe if Grandma Mueller played, I might've put her into bankruptcy. If that happened, she would've stuck my head in the downstairs toilet and pulled the chain.

I knew about that toilet from a previous visit. It was in a little room off the hallway past the kitchen, on the way out the back door. It was so old it should've been in the Plumber's Museum. Way up high over the seat was a wooden tank full of water. There was a long chain coming down from the tank. To flush it, you pulled on the chain. Trouble was, that always brought water from the box dripping down all over you.

We played the steeplechase game twice. After trying another ridiculous game, we got bored and started looking around the house. We tip-toed upstairs and went exploring through the bedrooms. In Grandma's bedroom, we found a chamber pot under her bed. This was hard to understand at first, what with the toilet downstairs.

Then I remembered the water from that wooden tank. It wouldn't be much fun sitting on the stool, getting dripped on and then going back upstairs to bed in a wet nightie.

Another bedroom upstairs was used by our cousin, Danielle, when she had lived there as a little girl—years before Skipper and I came along. It looked like her bedroom was kept just as she left it, like some kind of a shrine. The wallpaper was flowery and the bedspread had pictures of plump little angels. There was even a little toy piano with keys that played when you pushed them. Danielle was the only child of Uncle Henry, a doctor over in Canyon City. Uncle Henry was Mom's favorite brother. Since Skipper was always pretending to be such a four-square upright do-gooder, she figured he would turn out like Uncle Henry. She said her other brother, Uncle Erik, was a good-for-nothing slacker. She said I would turn out like Uncle Erik.

Out behind Grandma's house was a woodshed smelling of paint and sawdust—the workshop and hideout of Uncle Erik. It seemed to me like he got a bum rap from Mom. He never hurt anybody, far as I know, and he wasn't lazy. Every time we went to Grandma's house, we found him out in the woodshed repairing a table or painting a chair. He was a handyman. You could call him an onta-pra-newer. He fixed things for people and seemed to have quite a following. He always made Skipper and me feel at home, a big relief after the crappy welcome we got from Grandma.

Uncle Erik was shorter than Dad, with combed-over black hair, a small moustache and a gap in his front teeth which showed when he smiled. He went to college a couple years, and everybody hoped he would be an insurance agent or a real estate guy or maybe even a bank clerk. Something respectable. But he seemed completely happy being independent and free from any hassles, just doing handyman work. He wasn't a drunk and he never got thrown in jail. He did get married once. Some lady over on the west side of town got her hooks in him. She swept him off his feet and got him to marry her. She stayed with him for a while and then filed for divorce. I think she figured he had some big bucks stashed away and I think she went to a lot of trouble for nothing.

~ * ~

Back in Redmond, Skipper and I knew better than to let Mom know we were feeling sick. Her mother—Grandma Mueller—had been a midwife and helped her husband run a drug store back in the day. That made her some kind of phony medical expert. She had taught Mom all the Victorian remedies and Mom was eager to apply this state-of-the-art science to a captive audience of two—me and Skipper. Whenever I got sick, I was put to bed with the window shades drawn to make it dark. Then she hooked up some crummy vaporizer to send up clouds of steam loaded with camphor oil.

That wasn't hard to take. But in the next step, Mom spread a layer of mustard goop on my chest and covered it with a thick itchy cloth that heated me up so much I could hardly breathe. After that, you better get well or else. Because the next step after that was just plain unspeakable. The next step was to be avoided at all costs. No matter how bad I felt, I always tried to show that I was really okay. I tried to swallow any trace of sneezing and stifle any hint of coughing. Because the next step was the ultimate sure-fire Mueller Solution. The next step was the dreaded enema.

It's difficult to describe this stupid procedure, but a dictionary says it's the "injection of liquid into the intestine by way of the anus." Simple and easy, right? Not in a thousand years. It's painful and humiliating. And especially painful and humiliating for a kid who had no say on whether to raise the fearful tank to a high point and unhook the terrifying red rubber hose.

There are powerful forces of nature at work here, much like those created when a dam is constructed across a major river. When engineers plan a hydro-electric dam, they talk about the gigantic forces of falling water. They speak in awed tones of something called the "head" of water which comes surging down with enormous pressure to spin giant turbines and generate millions of kilowatts of electricity for cities throughout the region.

Something akin to that power is unleashed when you elevate a one-gallon container of saltwater connected by a rubber hose to the innards of a ten-year-old boy. When the hand-clip is released, the Law of Hydraulics is unleashed to an unspeakable degree of upwelling and purging, which no strong man can bear to witness. After a few times on the receiving end of this cutting-edge technology, Skipper and I learned to choke back any sniffles, hide any sneezing and stifle any complaints. We always forced ourselves, no matter how sick, to get up and go to school and try to survive until the ailment had healed itself. This record of perfect health convinced Mom that the Mueller Solution was the ultimate answer to any childhood affliction. She always kept the contraption sitting high on a bathroom shelf, its red rubber hose and long black insertion tube dangling against the bathroom wall in the most threatening manner possible.

~ * ~

One of my friends at school was a kid named Jake Hartley. He was round-faced and freckled and wore the same bib overalls and plaid shirt every day. Old Hartley was always good-natured, even when some of the kids called him an "Okie." His family had come out from Oklahoma and they lived just west of town, Jake said. He invited me home for supper one time. I had told Mom about it, so I went home with him straight after school. When we got to the edge of Dry Canyon, I asked him where his place was.

"Over yonder," he said, pointing to a tarpaper shack in a pasture-like spot of grass in the shallow canyon.

Over yonder. I had never heard that word spoken, but I knew what he meant. His house was down there where he pointed. We took a trail into the canyon and followed a dirt path along a barbed-wire fence. We came to a gate, just a post secured by wire loops at the top and at the ground. Hartley opened the gate and let me in, then put the post back in the loops. We walked over to his house. The outside walls were covered with tarpaper. That meant they didn't have enough money for siding to finish the job. But the place looked like it could stand up in a storm. He got some pellets out of a gunny sack and fed them to some white rabbits in cages stacked up along the house.

We went inside. Hartley introduced me to his pa, ma and his kid sister, Eloise. Then we sat down and had some supper. It wasn't too bad. We had carrots, bread, and some fried meat which tasted like chicken. I figured it was one of those cute little bunny rabbits in the cages outside. I could see they didn't have any electricity. They used a wood stove to heat water and warm the place. They had some kerosene lamps to light after dark. They drew water from a well with a pump handle and they had an outhouse over by the garden. To wash clothes, Jake said, his mother used a big metal tub and washboard and hung the stuff on a clothes-line to dry. His father didn't have a job yet, but he was trying hard to find one. The good news was, they had escaped the Dust Bowl and were in beautiful Oregon. And they had somehow built this place. It wasn't a palace, but it wasn't too bad. Besides, with all those rabbits and a garden full of carrots and potatoes, I could see they weren't going to starve any time soon.

I knew the talk downtown was against the Okies moving in and taking jobs away from the locals. I heard this talk once when Dad took me along to the hardware store. I felt kinda guilty about it, but I was on the side of the Okies. I thought they were really good people who just needed a break. They reminded me, in fact, of the pioneers who crossed the plains in covered wagons.

In Oregon, pioneers are remembered as saints or demi-gods, from exhibits showing the pioneers crossing thousands of miles of grasslands and deserts and over mountains to reach this Promised Land. In songs, books and movies, they're proclaimed as heroic frontiersmen and empire-builders. They're enshrined by bronze statues in city parks and marble sculptures at the State Capitol. Okies as pioneers, that's how I saw them.

I got the idea from Hartley's front door. It didn't have a regular doorknob or lock. It had a simple iron latch inside, pulled on the outside by rawhide straps through a hole in the door. At night, you just pulled in the latchstring to lock up. It was ingenious, something the pioneers would have done. In fact, Hartley's place was probably a lot like the first pioneer homes. I thought maybe, in a hundred years or so, some rich guy might get the same idea. He might understand how the Okies had pulled off another great migration to reach this Eden called Oregon. Maybe he would see that the Okies deserved a statue, too. Somewhere in a city park, maybe that rich guy would pay for a bronze statue of some Okies, a whole family, crossing the plains in a beat-up old rattletrap Ford truck.

~ * ~

There was a girl named Sarah Whittaker who lived a couple blocks north of my house. We had the same birthday, so we had some birthday parties together. She said we were "soul-mates" and we had to be nice to each other. I thought that was a bunch of nonsense, but I didn't argue about it. She was okay as a soul-mate—whatever that was—but I didn't see her as a girlfriend one little bit. She was tall, scrawny and kind of gawky, if you know what I mean. I just tried to get along with her. But then she wanted to stage a mock wedding, with her and me as the bride and groom. That idea made me as happy as getting my tonsils pulled out. It gave me the creeps, in fact, big time. But she kept harping on it so much, I just caved in. I figured no harm could come of it. I figured wrong.

Before I knew it, she had built this thing into the biggest Metro-Goldwyn-Mayer production you ever saw. Her mother thought the idea was kinda cute and really got into the act. She sewed up a white bridal dress for Sarah and she sewed me a stupid kind of formal get-up, like Fred Astaire, with white shirt, tie, and fancy coat and pants. Everything except a top hat.

In the time before the big event, I tried to forget about it. I had enough problems worrying about the Mexican and those playing cards. But the days kept rolling by until they finally got to the Saturday I had been dreading. Desolate and depressed, I climbed on my bike and rode over to her house. I was filled with a sense of doom, helpless to ward off my fate. When I got there, I saw her place was packed with kids who had come over to see this phony show and feast on tons of ice cream and cake.

I parked my bike by the garage, went in the back door and into the bedroom where my stupid costume was waiting. I had no choice but to put it on. Then I went out to the back yard. It was swarming with kids, laughing and running around. Some of them were sitting on folding chairs lined up in proper rows like pews at church. Up front was a small altar, built by Sarah's daddy from plywood and painted a shiny dark brown. The whole set-up seemed almost like a real church. I walked up to the front and stood there before the altar, a lamb waiting to be slaughtered.

Suddenly I heard her mother banging away on the piano inside. From some movie, I knew it was a wedding march. Then the bride appeared in all her white splendor, walking real slow, grinning and handing off little waves to the audience, milking this phony scene for all it was worth. I just stood there in front of everybody, helpless, waiting for the executioner.

Finally, Sarah got up to the altar and gave me a big toothy grin. As we stood there, she grabbed my hand. She grabbed so hard, it hurt like crazy. She had a real strong grip and wouldn't let up one little bit.

Then a guy came out from behind a hedge and walked up to us. It was that phony Borden Turnbow, two years older and a preacher's kid. He was dressed up like a real preacher, too, with a black suit, white shirt and a cheesy tie. He carried a big Bible which he placed on the altar. His round red face was flushed with importance, and he had a look of great and serious endeavors. This was no joke to him; I could see that real plain. It was no joke to me either.

That Turnbow had a script to read and he followed it line by line, every single word, with a heavy-handed tone as solemn and as deadly as a judge sentencing a defendant to death row.

"Dearly Beloved, we are gathered here today in the presence of friends and family, to give recognition to the worth and beauty of love, and to add our blessings to the words which shall unite bride and groom in holy matrimony…"

I was starting to feel light-headed. I felt like I might pass out any second. This was way more serious than anything I had imagined. It was starting to look like I was gonna get hooked for good!

"…friends, we have gathered here to share with Sarah and Hamilton a most important moment of their lives. Their love and mutual understanding have grown and ripened, and now they have decided to live their lives as husband and wife…"

Baloney! I sure never decided to live my life that way!! I got real shaky in the knees and felt like I was gonna keel over any second.

"...a husband and wife should not confuse love of worldly goods with love of one another...(blah—blah—blah)...the measure of true love is love freely given and freely accepted...(blah, blah, blah)..."

All this time, I kept staring at that Bible sitting there on the altar. It was a big one, almost too big for that little plywood altar to hold up, a real Bible that Turnbow had brought from his old man's church. It seemed to have a power all its own—this book with its soft black leather covers which folded down over the edges and with a long black tassel coming down from the top to keep track of the page. A terrible thought dawned on me. With this real Bible on the altar and with a real preacher's kid doing the talking, well, maybe I was really getting hitched!

"Oh, crap!"

I got sick to my stomach and felt real dizzy, like I would drop over any second. I took a deep breath and tried to think of something nice, say, a chocolate ice cream cone. Sarah crushed my hand in hers, the sudden pain shooting me back to reality. Old Turnbow began asking stupid questions. Each time, I mumbled, "I do," in a voice so low you could barely hear it. And each time, Sarah flashed that sickening grin and proclaimed, "I Do!" in a voice so loud you could hear it downtown.

I stared at the Bible again, wondering if my goose was getting cooked for good. Then Turnbow asked me a question. I was staring at the Bible so hard I didn't hear him. Everything came to a screeching halt.

Sarah gave me a jab to wake me up. Turnbow looked at me like I was a total moron.

"Do you take this woman to be your lawfully wedded wife?"

I wanted to run away, run away fast to some place far away. But I was in too deep now to back out. "I do," I mumbled, with a feeling I might puke any second.

He looked at Sarah. "Do you take this man to be your lawfully wedded husband?" She flashed that big toothy grin and proclaimed "I do!" in a very loud voice.

How long can this misery go on? I asked myself that over and over as Turnbow droned on about this holy sacrament, about the sanctity of marriage and some other putrid baloney he had stuffed in his script. Then suddenly he drew himself up to his full height and said, "I Now Pronounce You Man and Wife. You May Now Kiss the Bride."

Without warning, Sarah grabbed me, spun me around and planted a big watery kiss right on my mouth. A big urge to barf washed over me like a wave. I felt like I was gonna puke for sure. But finally she pulled away. I took a couple of real deep breaths, like Mom told me once when I got carsick.

Then Sarah's mother started banging away on her stupid piano, a tune that meant I was cooked for good. Old Sarah just stood there in front of the crowd, gripping my hand harder than ever, waving with the other hand, grinning like an idiot. Nobody knew what to do next. Then some kids ran over to the table for the cake and ice cream. Sarah chased after them, trying to keep them from fighting over the food. All of a sudden, the coast was clear.

I ran into the back bedroom where my clothes were. I tore off the costume, put on my regular clothes and ran out the back door. Nobody saw me escape. I ran behind the garage and jumped on my bike. I took off fast as I could, riding down back alleys in a kind of wide circular pattern in case they came out looking for me.

Once I made it home, I breathed a big sigh of relief and hid my bike inside the garage. Feeling better, I ran inside the house and turned on the radio. I sat there and stared at that wonderful old floor-model Philco with its soothing yellow light behind the line you moved to change stations. I didn't even care what program was on. I was safe at home again and free from my scary encounter with Sarah and Reverend Borden Turnbow and the sacred institution of marriage.

~ * ~

One evening, Dad said his workers had brought in a stray dog somebody had dumped off on the Bend highway. He said the dog was tied up over at the truck maintenance shed. After dinner, I walked down to his office and went out back to the shed. There I found the most pitiful animal I had ever seen. He was a German shepherd, fully grown but almost starved. He was wet and shivering from the cold and his eyes were dull and lifeless. His ears were drooping, tail between his legs, and he whimpered slightly as I went up to him. I petted his wet head and he looked up, surprised at this small act of kindness.

I stroked his head for a minute, then made a sudden decision. I untied him. He looked at me again, somewhat confused. I petted him again and his tail wagged just a little.

"C'mon, boy, follow me," I said. He followed me home, dutifully walking several steps behind. When we got home, I went through our garbage can and dug out the remains of a roast beef dinner. He wolfed it down, now and then looking up at me m a grateful way. I got more leftovers from the garbage to feed him. Then I found some plywood and made a lean-to shelter against the garage. I filled the shelter with rags for him to sleep on. I set out a bowl of water and he lapped it up. Then he crawled into his new home and fell into a deep sleep.

Next day, I got Mom to buy some regular dog food. Then, every day I fed him and petted him and kept his bowl full of water. Before long, his body had filled out. His coat was sleek and his eyes were clear and shining. I called him Wimpy. It didn't mean he was a wimp. He was named after Popeye's buddy in the funnies. Wimpy was no wimp, for sure.

He followed me everywhere. He followed me to school and waited for me all day. Soon as I came outside, he jumped up and ran over to me, tail wagging like crazy, eyes looking up eagerly for approval. He followed me when I walked downtown to the movies. He laid down outside the theater, patiently waiting three hours for the movie to finish, just lying there on the sidewalk next to the building. When I came out, he jumped up and ran over to me, tail wagging, eyes eagerly seeking mine. Often he licked my hand. On the way home, he walked alongside me, tail wagging. Now and then he glanced up at me with shining eyes, panting happily, looking at me like I was King of the Universe.

There was one great benefit to having Wimpy. If the Mexican ever showed up, I knew Wimpy would sacrifice his life to save me. He was a police dog, a German shepherd. His ancestors had bred them over many generations to guard their masters and ward off suspicious intruders. He felt that was his job and he took his job very seriously.

Wimpy knew he had to tolerate Skipper, no matter what. But if anyone else came near me, watch out. He figured it was his job to defend me, and defend me he did. It happened on the way to school and it happened on the way home. If any kid got too close to me, he jumped up and knocked him down. He never bit anybody, he just knocked them down. Then, of course, the kid got up and ran home crying. It wasn't long before Wimpy became famous in town as a vicious beast on the loose, a Hound of the Baskervilles, a monster lurking in dark alleys waiting to prey on innocent children. He became a target of vengeance by a mob of angry and blood-thirsty parents.

If Dad and Mom had given this crisis more thought, maybe they could've come up with a solution. Maybe Wimpy could've been sent to a dog trainer. Maybe taken out to a ranch someplace, to someone who would value a good watchdog. But events moved too fast. As a state employee, Dad had to think about political fallout over in Salem. And so the die was cast. One evening, Dad said the cops were coming for Wimpy.

When the cops pulled up in their patrol car, Wimpy started barking like crazy. When they got out, he went berserk. He barked and lunged at them, snapping his jaws, hairs on his back standing straight up. The cops jumped back in their car. Quite a little crowd had gathered around.

"Get the kid in the back seat," somebody yelled. "The dog will follow him in there!"

I looked at Dad and he nodded. I was heart-broken. But I was trapped. There was no way out. I could run away and Wimpy would come with me. But the cops would follow us and we'd soon be back in the same boat. So I opened the back door and got in. Wimpy stopped barking. Tail wagging, he jumped in alongside me, eager for some new adventure. I stroked his head and looked him in the eye and kissed him on the nose. Then I got out the other side and shut the door. The cops took off. Wimpy looked out the back window, surprised that I wasn't going with him.

I raced in the house, ran to my bedroom and flung myself on the bed. I knew what they were going to do. They were going to take

Wimpy out in the desert. They were going to stop and let him out. Then they were going to shoot him dead. Lousy damned grownups, killing my dog like that. And I was the Judas who had betrayed him, who led him to his slaughter. After that, I never wanted another dog. Never again.

~ * ~

A few weeks after, a friend said his older brother needed some kids to sell copies of *Saturday Evening Post* magazines by going door-to-door. I decided to sign up for it. I did it partly to take my mind off Wimpy. And because I read someplace that every big-time onta-pranewer started out this way. And I did it because I was tired of begging Mom for money every time I wanted to go see a movie.

Whatever the reason, I went ahead and tried it. It left a lasting impression. Whenever I hear about the painter Norman Rockwell, I see huge stacks of those stupid magazines I was supposed to sell.

The magazines came in each Saturday, a big pile of them all demanding to be taken door-to-door and peddled for a nickel. Each week, I untied my bundle with a reluctant sigh. Then I put the magazines in my bike basket and rode out into the streets with a feeling of hopeless despair. Each week, I stopped first at the grade school playground—perhaps longing for a return to carefree student days—and sat down to examine my goods.

It was always the same cover, a Norman Rockwell painting behind the words *Saturday Evening Post* and always about ordinary stuff. One week, the painting showed guys singing barbershop songs in a real barbershop. Another week, the cover showed a teen-age boy and girlfriend riding around in a car's rumble seat. Those Rockwell covers were about regular life, real life situations in America as we were living it. Of course, none of those covers showed a pathetic little kid trying to peddle a magazine called *Saturday Evening Post*.

When I finally got myself ready to go selling, I worked up a little routine to get me through the agony. First, I told myself that it would take about ten turn-downs or door-slams before anybody actually bought the stupid magazine. Second, I got myself into a kind of trance. It was a sort of out-ofbody experience, the real me standing away somewhere else and watching myself from a distance. So I would walk up to a house and hit the doorbell. When the lady came to the door, I would hold out the magazine and ask if she wanted to buy it.

Hearing "no," I would go on to the next house, and ask the same question and wait for the "no" and go on to the next house. I did this over and over with the idea that ten "no" answers would finally produce a "yes" reply. Here's the important part—it wasn't me going through all this misery. It was some other kid, a poor jerk who looked just like me. The real me was standing on the sidewalk, watching this pitiful spectacle with a contemptuous smirk on my face.

Then one Saturday, something totally unexpected happened to my "double." It was so unexpected and so good that I fired my "double" right on the spot.

It happened at a house on a street about half-way between my place and Dry Canyon. The house was one-level, like most of them around town. It was light brown, with a big tree in the front yard and a driveway running alongside the house leading to a single-car garage. Not a trace of anything to say this house was in any way unusual. It was a standard house. In fact, it looked a lot like my house. Commonplace. Just an ordinary house on a typical street. But what happened there knocked me for a loop. As my "double," I took two steps up to the concrete landing and rang the doorbell. A lady opened the door. She looked at me and drew back in surprise.

"Aren't you Douglas Skutt's son?" she asked.

I nodded.

"I'm Marge Dunham," she announced proudly. "My husband works for your daddy!"

"Would you like to buy a *Saturday Evening Post*? Only a nickel."

"For you, of course! Just a moment!" She ran to get her purse and ran back holding out the nickel as a sort of trophy. I took it, gave her a magazine and we just stood there grinning at each other. By then, I had entirely forgotten about my "double." He was fired and down the road. I had crawled back into my own skin and was my old self again.

"Do you know any other Highway people around here?"

"Yes, of course! Just a moment!" She ran into the living room and grabbed an address book and came back to the front door. "They're all in here," she said, holding up the book. "I'll write them all down for you!"

I stood there in a kind of stupor, giddy with this incredible windfall, this legendary act of falling in a cesspool and coming up roses. She wrote out the names and addresses of eight Highway employees and handed the paper to me. I took it like I was receiving a treasure map—eight households willing to give the boss's son a nickel for a magazine—and the master key to untold riches. At last I was on my way to becoming a real onta-pra-newer!

I mumbled a "thanks" to my benefactor as I waved goodbye and walked on a cloud to my bike. Holding this precious document that would no doubt change my life forever, I put the paper ever so carefully in my pants pocket and sped off down the street.

I peddled directly to the first house on the list. When the lady came to the door, I called her by name and introduced myself. I told her that Marge Jenkins had given me her name when she bought a magazine. Of course, the second lady also bought a magazine. My new system worked on the third lady and fourth lady and all the other ladies on the list. I sold almost all of my magazines to the ladies of the Highway Department and could look forward to future sales each and every week!

In the thrill and excitement of this bonanza, I decided to come up with a name for my new operation. For some reason, I remembered tales of mountain men trapping beavers during early frontier days. I remembered how they set out traps in many streams and lakes. They called this system a "trap line" for their string of traps to catch the beavers. I decided to call my new system a "trap line" in honor of those mountain men who were my mentors and inspiration. As a modern mountain man, I decided to celebrate my good fortune by attending a movie. No need to beg Mom. Skipper, of course, happily begged for his admission money and came along without any qualms.

Each Saturday after that, I took my magazines directly to each Highway Department house and sold one to each lady. My trap line was paying off handsomely. I knew I had finally stumbled onto the secret of business, the master key to becoming a real onta-pranewer—"it ain't what ya know, it's who ya know!"

Six

Several weeks later, the local newspaper had a story on the front page. It said Ma Fisher was sponsoring a contest for kids to win a brand-new Schwinn bicycle. It said she would give out the details at 10:30 next Saturday morning at her drug store. On Saturday morning, I got my magazines as usual. But I didn't go out to sell them right away. Instead, I went down to Fisher's Drug Store to hear all about the contest.

A whole bunch of kids were milling around inside the store. Ma Fisher rang a little bell to get our attention and climbed up on a chair so we could see her okay. She was short and plump, with a mop of red hair like a clown's wig. She had some new Elixir of Youth, just arrived from New York City, available to Redmond patrons for the first time ever. I wondered why she didn't try some on herself. She said she was going to sponsor a contest which would last for one month. Kids in the contest would go door-to-door selling these bottles for fifty cents each. You started with four bottles. When you sold those and brought in the two dollars, you got four coupons. At the end of the contest, the kid holding the most coupons won the contest and got the bike.

She turned and gestured and some guy wheeled out the brand-new Schwinn bicycle. All the kids yelled and whistled at the sight. She asked who wanted to enter the contest. I threw up my hands and so did most of the other kids. Then we all got in line to pick up our bottles. While waiting, I could hardly keep from grinning. I was secretly rubbing my hands together, thinking about my trap-line. I knew I could get rid of four bottles easy. Add another four bottles from, hopefully, the other employees and I would have eight coupons. I figured most kids would get discouraged after a few days of getting turned down. If I sold just eight bottles, I figured, I would win the bike. I quit the magazine selling job and devoted all my attention to my new cosmetics line. I now had much bigger fish to fry.

As I hoped, each Highway wife was willing to part with fifty cents to buy a bottle of this Elixir of Youth and keep the boss's son happy. By the end of the second week, I had reached my goal of eight coupons. All I had to do was wait for the contest to finish. I worried a lot about keeping my coupons safe from Skipper. I was afraid he might throw them in the garbage, just to get even for some imaginary injury he had suffered from me. I desperately needed a place to keep them absolutely safe for the two weeks left in the contest.

Finally, I decided to put them in a little bowl on the fireplace mantel in the living room. Skipper wouldn't dare screw around with them there. I looked at them fondly each day, my precious little coupons, waiting patiently for the contest to run out, waiting for that glorious day when Ma Fisher would hand over my brand-new Schwinn bicycle.

One night, after riding my bike all day, I climbed up on a chair to check on my coupons. I couldn't believe it—they were gone!

"Hey, Mom," I said, "what happened to my coupons?'

She gave me a saintly little smile. "I had a visit today from a dear lady at church. I think you know her—Mrs. Nordquist?"

Yeah, so what? I said to myself.

"She told me about her son, Byron."

Yeah, I know that jerk, Byron Nordquist. So what?

She said Byron had entered the contest sponsored by Fisher Drug Store. He had gone all over town and hadn't sold a single bottle. She said her son was upset and discouraged and wouldn't listen to any words of consolation. She was worried sick that her son would get an inferiority complex.

I felt a sudden panic, an awful premonition of disaster, a foreboding of doom. "So you gave away my coupons?"

Mom smiled again, a serene and beatific smile, one reflecting all the blessings of heaven from earthly good works. "Yes, I gave her the coupons. I felt it was my Christian duty to help. To help her son. So he wouldn't get an inferiority complex."

How about your Christian duty to help me? How about my inferiority complex? I didn't say those words; I just thought them. Truth is, I was too shocked to say anything. All I could do was imagine that phony Byron Nordquist riding around on *my* Schwinn, enjoying all the fruits of *my* scheming and *my* hard work! I was devastated. But it taught me something: All grownups are crooks. And all your plotting, conniving and hard work is meaningless if your mom is willing to give you the shaft?

I had dreamed about becoming an onta-pra-newer, But then I decided maybe it wasn't such a hot deal after all. No great plans, no great disappointments. I thought maybe I should just become a handyman. Like Uncle Erik.

~ * ~

When I returned to school from summer vacation, I discovered that our new teacher was a good-looking lady, about twenty-five, with reddish blonde hair and a trim little figure in a tailored woman's suit and the sweetest manner you could ever imagine. Her name was Charlotte Ward. She looked like the kind of lady Dad would call "spiffy." She was so gorgeous she took my breath away. She made me forget all about my problems with old Mr. Philpott the year before.

School settled down into the routine of arithmetic, geography, spelling, reading, and all the other grade school stuff. From week to week, I worked myself ragged keeping my school studies and homework up-to-date and doing everything possible to impress the fabulous Miss Ward. I longed for a smile, perhaps even a wink, anything to let me know my hard work was appreciated. But, I was treated exactly as everyone else—even those who fell behind in their work—and I sometimes wondered if she was even aware of my existence.

Then one morning, Miss Ward made an announcement. She said the Women's Christian Temperance Union was sponsoring an essay contest. Everyone in the class was expected to enter. The WCTU ladies would come to our classroom the following week to explain.

Next Monday morning, three old ladies were standing in front of the blackboard when I went into the classroom. At a nod by Miss Ward, one of them talked about the contest and how important it was to write a good essay. She said the essay contest would be about the evils of drinking booze. Only she didn't call it booze. She called it spirits. That killed me, spirits. She said they would hand out a booklet to give us some ideas about what to write. While she was talking, the other two walked around passing out copies of the booklet. I looked at mine. It had lots of stuff about the evils of drinking spirits and many drawings of bottles labeled "John Barleycorn." The first lady said she knew Miss Ward would like to have a good essay from each one of us. Then she and the others walked out.

At first, I didn't much care about their shabby old essay contest. But then I thought about Miss Ward and how I could impress her by winning the contest. Yes, I thought, that would really do the trick.

So I set out to write the best essay anyone could possibly write about the evils of drinking John Barleycorn. I thought long and hard about this subject and what I could say about it. From my imagination, I dredged up all kinds of crazy stuff. I described a man with a wife and five kids who blows his paycheck at the local saloon and winds up dead-drunk under a pool table. I told of a mother who couldn't leave booze alone and ends up drowning her kids in the bathtub. I drew on personal experience. I described a man, college graduate, a pillar of the community and a member of the Masonic Lodge, who hides a bottle of wine in the kitchen and swigs it down while his wife is asleep. In my concluding narrative, I made a solemn vow that no such vile and corrupt spirits would ever touch my lips. I swore an oath that if I were in a saloon and some man offered to buy me a drink of John

Barleycorn, well sir, then I would thrash that man within an inch of his life.

I finished my essay and showed it to Miss Ward. I had hoped to gain a smile, perhaps, or at least some tiny recognition of my valiant effort. But she seemed detached and even a bit annoyed at dealing with this essay contest. I didn't understand that, but I was used to her cool reserve. So I shrugged, handed in my essay and forgot about it.

A month later, the WCTU announced that it would name the essay contest winner at a special ceremony that Friday after school at the Redmond High School gymnasium. The WCTU stated that all school officials were expected to attend—all the principals and teachers, the school board, the mayor and city council, plus any other politicians who hoped to survive the next election. Everybody was expected to show up and everybody did.

If you really want to know—first prize went to yours truly, Hamilton Skutt. Whoop-te-do! Okay, so I didn't get a cash prize or a trophy, or even a plaque to hang on the wall. There was a certificate, I think, but it got lost in the shuffle. I didn't even get my essay back as a keepsake. Somebody said they sent it to the national office to be copied and sent out as a perfect example of what they were looking for. I didn't get a single thing out of it, not one thin dime. But what happened was better than any prize.

I was going to attend this big awards ceremony after school on Friday like everyone else. But on my way over there, I saw some guys playing baseball. That looked like more fun, so I joined in the game.

Meanwhile, back at the gym, the place was filling up with school board members, principals, teachers, politicians, mothers, WCTU members, and everybody else who had nothing better to do. The high school band played a few rousing numbers to get the crowd juiced. At a table in front of the stage, the mayor made a little welcoming speech and introduced the local WCTU president. She gave another welcoming speech. Then she pulled a slip of paper from her pocket and read the runner-up winner. A girl from my class, Doris Yoder, ran up and got her certificate and everyone clapped. Then the WCTU president held up her hand for silence. She waited a few seconds to milk all the suspense and get people sitting on the edge of their chairs. She reached into her pocket and brought forth another paper to finally unveil the first-prize winner. Then, with an air of profound consequence, she rendered the verdict:

"The Women's Christian Temperance Union proudly announces that the winner of the essay-writing competition on the evils of drinking alcoholic spirits is...Hamilton Skutt!"

There was a long silence. Nothing happened. She read my name again. More silence. People in the audience looked at each other. Where was the winner? The WCTU president looked embarrassed, almost panicky. The mayor took a long look at his watch as if to force time to go by quicker. The city council members looked at each other. The school board members shook their heads in disbelief. Then a little girl ran up to a teacher and whispered something. The teacher went up to the grade school principal and whispered something. The principal walked to the front of the gym and whispered something to the WCTU president. She pursed her lips in disgust and, it was said, looked like she could use a good stiff drink herself. Finally, she cleared her throat and addressed the assembled multitude:

"We understand the winner is playing baseball two blocks away."

Another long silence. Then a woman noticed Mom sitting in the audience. She motioned Mom to go up and get the prize. Several others picked up the idea and started waving at her and pointing to the front. A murmur of approval swept through the crowd. At first, Mom shook her head. Then, with a shy little smile, she stood up to a burst of applause. She worked her way across the row of spectators and up to the head table amidst more applause.

She accepted a manila envelope and took the microphone. She thanked the mayor for attending. She thanked the city council members for attending. She thanked the school board members for attending. She thanked the grade school principal and teachers for their fine instruction of her son. She said she was happy to accept the first prize on behalf of her son. Then she walked back to her row of seats amidst thunderous applause. It might have been the happiest day of her life.

Five Cards and a Cathouse

Like I said, that certificate got lost in the shuffle. But it didn't matter. And I really enjoyed the rest of the year as a well-behaved pupil of the lovely Miss Ward. At the end of the year, she announced her upcoming marriage to Blake Thornton. The school board had set up strict rules forbidding teachers from getting married. But Miss Ward wanted to keep teaching, even as Mrs. Thornton, so her future father-in-law got in the act. He was R. J. Thornton, owner of Thornton & Biggs, the local department store, and the town's kingfish. When he talked, people listened. With a couple of phone calls, he took care of that pesky no-get-married rule. After that, any woman teacher could get married anytime she wanted. Just so long as somebody asked her. As for the essay contest: it was an elaborate scheme, of course, to mold our innocent little minds into making us permanent teetotalers. More lousy grownups and their nasty tricks!

~ * ~

When summer arrived, Dad announced plans for another family vacation. This year, he said, we were going to drive all the way to San Francisco. We were going there to take in the San Francisco World's Fair.

About a week before we left, Dad came home one night with a brand-new 1939 Plymouth Road King. It was a black four-door, not as sexy as our old Studebaker Dictator, but with more passenger space. We needed that extra room for all six of us driving five hundred miles down there and back.

Finally, the day arrived for departure. We loaded up the Plymouth with all the suitcases in the trunk. Then we climbed in and took off. We headed south on Highway 97, past the great city of Bend, and kept going south through miles of Ponderosa pine.

We drove through the village of LaPine, near the turn-off for the road to East Lake. I looked at the few stores and houses scattered here and there. Could this be the place where the East Lake Girl lived? Why did I keep thinking she lived in LaPine? Would I ever see her again?

Going south along Highway 97, we motored through endless forests of pine, past little logging towns like Chemult and Pine Ridge, and finally got to Klamath Falls for lunch. We continued south. Then suddenly we crossed the state line, past a sign reading "Welcome To California."

A few miles down the road, we had to pull into a station where they checked to see if we had any fruit. Why they were so worried about us bringing in any fruit? Who knows? But, no big deal. Dad just said "no fruit" and they took his word for it. They didn't stand him up and frisk him or ransack the suitcases, or anything like that, just waved us on through.

At the town of Weed, we merged with Highway 99 and kept rolling along. After Dunsmuir, we dropped out of the mountains into the Sacramento Valley. We kept going, through Redding, and finally came to Red Bluff. It was hot and dry, like California was supposed to be. And palm trees! Not just a few, but dozens of the trees all over the place! Dad drove around town and found a motel overlooking the Sacramento River. We got unloaded and went out for dinner. Afterward, we went back and turned in for the night.

Next morning, I got up early and got dressed. I wanted to go outside and explore the place. I shook Skipper awake and motioned for him to come with me. But as usual he didn't want to make any waves and stayed behind. I tip-toed around the place and opened the door slow and easy, so as not to wake anybody, and stepped outside.

For a while, I walked around a few blocks just admiring the town. Then I went down to the Sacramento River and walked along the shoreline. I saw a large rock just off the bank. I jumped over to that rock. There was another rock further out, so I jumped onto that rock. Then another rock and another jump. Another rock and another jump. Before long, I reached a slice of land right out in the middle of the river. I felt like Robinson Crusoe. Or Blackbeard, the pirate. Then I heard somebody yelling. I looked across the river and saw Dad, Mom and Skipper standing on the shoreline. "How in hell did you get over on that island?" Dad yelled. "Come back right now!" Skipper just looked and smiled as if to say, "Look what a mess you got yourself into now!"

It wasn't any trouble getting back. I jumped from one rock to another—reversing the way I had come over—then jumped off on the shore and smiled as if to say, "No harm done." But they weren't buying it. "Crazy kid!" muttered Dad, storming off in a trail of cigar smoke.

After everybody loaded their stuff, Dad fired up the Plymouth and we took off. Heading south again, Dad had that pissed-off look he gets sometime and Mom wasn't too friendly, either. Skipper was slunk down over by the window looking smug and pleased with himself. What the hell did I do that was so wrong? Just jumped a few rocks and got out in the middle of the stupid river. Was that such a big crime?

We rolled south through Willows and other little towns along the Sacramento Valley. One thing for sure—we found out what real heat felt like. I thought we would never get away from that part of the state, with all the irrigated fields and millions of tiny bugs plastered all over the stupid windshield.

We came to a little town where Dad left the main highway and followed a different road promising a shortcut to San Francisco. Not long after, it started cooling off real fast. We left the steaming valley and drove between hills of yellow grass, straight toward a huge cloud bank. Upon reaching the cloud, we drove into a world of fog and cool air and kept rolling along and came to Vallejo. We were on the outer edges of San Francisco Bay. It was so misty Dad had to turn on the windshield wipers. They slurped back and forth, mixing up a stew of bugs and water.

We drove past a continuous string of scummy stores, houses, and gas stations and finally came into Berkeley, and then Oakland. It was getting late, so Dad pulled into a sleazy little motel for the night. Each of us found a bed to sleep on. We walked a couple blocks to a greasy-spoon cafe for some dinner before turning in for the night.

Next morning, I woke up to the sound of screaming. I looked up and saw Evelyn and Veronica yelling, creaming, slamming wet towels on everything. The place was alive with millions of ants crawling over the floors and walls. Mom had us pack up in a hurry and get the hell out of there as fast as we could.

We followed a divided boulevard for a while, then drove right onto the San Francisco-Oakland Bay Bridge. Dad said it was a suspension bridge. He pointed out the huge cables, thick as old-growth fir trees, running over the top of the high black towers holding up smaller cables which held up the bridge platform. He drove us across the bridge and we went down onto the streets of San Francisco. Awesome! We had arrived! Dad took a right and worked his way through traffic to Market Street and down to Embarcadero and along the waterfront to Fisherman's Wharf. He found a motor lodge nearby and we checked in. Each of us grabbed our stuff and ran inside to claim a bed. Then we got back in the car so Dad could drive us around the city.

What a city! We followed a winding street up Telegraph Hill, then came down and drove through Chinatown. The place seemed to be all hills covered with hotels and office buildings. Little cable cars came along, loaded with people inside and outside, their bells clanging away. On top of Nob Hill, we saw two famous hotels—the Mark Hopkins and Fairmont—sitting at the very summit of incredible glamour and excitement.

Dad drove us past the Civic Center and headed west, straight out on a street that took us to Golden Gate Park. That was the biggest park I had ever seen, zillions of acres of grass, trees, and lakes, right in the middle of this city of multi-story houses stuffed into every square foot.

Somebody mentioned the 1906 earthquake and I remembered the movie *San Francisco*. This park must've been the place where Clark Gable found Jeanette MacDonald, along with all the others running away from roaring fires and falling buildings of that earthquake. I was thinking about the movie and all the stuff that happened here as Dad drove out of the park and pulled up into the parking lot of a restaurant sitting on a bluff overlooking the Pacific. We had dinner there and drove back to our motor lodge at Fisherman's Wharf.

The next morning after breakfast, we all piled into the car and drove back onto the Bay Bridge. About half-way across, Dad pulled off and followed a ramp under the bridge and down onto Treasure Island. At last we had arrived at the San Francisco World's Fair!

It was fantastic, all kinds of exotic buildings stretching out in all directions. We got out and followed a broad sidewalk to the entrance.

Dad bought the admission tickets and we went inside. We came to a broad plaza loaded with benches. In the middle was a big pool with lots of fountains spurting water high into the air. Everybody agreed this would be the family meeting place. Evelyn and Veronica wanted to see the fair on their own. So Dad told them to meet everybody here at the fountains at six o'clock sharp. They said "okay" and took off.

Then Dad and Mom walked us all over the place. For hours and hours. Good thing they had a map to follow or we would've been up the creek. We started out from the Court of Honor, with its Tower of the Sun, headed south along the Avenue of the Seven Seas and came to Port of the Trade Winds. After that, we took in the Court of the East which led to the Lake of All Nations. Still later, we walked along the Court of Pacific which led to the Cavalcade of the Golden West.

For sure, this world's fair had lots of jazzy buildings, flashy plazas, splashy fountains and streets with super-fancy names.

The San Francisco World's Fair was supposed to promote peace in the world, at least around the Pacific. There was an eighty-foot-high statue of a goddess called "Pacifica" to symbolize peace in the Pacific. Each country had an exhibit to promote this idea of peace. I told Skipper the peace prize should go to the Japanese Pavilion. It had a huge pagoda with rooms full of geisha girls in colorful kimonos spinning silk. I had no doubt Japan should win first prize as the best promoter of peace in the Pacific. What a bunch of stupidity that was!

One morning, we watched in awe as a China Clipper, a giant flying boat, made a long takeoff from San Francisco Bay and slowly rose into the sky. It made a long and majestic turn and headed west over the Golden Gate Bridge, bound for Hawaii, Midway, Wake Island, Guam, Manila and Hong Kong—all of those fabled and faraway places in the peaceful Pacific Ocean. Peaceful at least for a while.

I think Dad and Mom finally got tired of dragging two kids around. On the third day, they plunked me and Skipper in a big movie theater with continuous movies about the glorious history of California. We saw movies about the Pony Express and movies about the Mexican War, movies about pioneers coming West in covered wagons, movies about Sutter's Mill and the Forty-Niners Gold Rush, movies about building the Western Pacific Railroad over the nasty Sierra Nevada mountains to link up with the Union Pacific. We learned a lot about California history, more than we really wanted to know.

When the folks finally came back to get us, it was late in the afternoon. On the way back to meet up with Evelyn and Veronica, we took a shortcut through a glorified carnival called the Gayway. We walked along through the crowds, sometimes bumping into other people out for a good time. Then I saw a sign:

SALLY RAND NUDE RANCH
WORLD'S MOST BEAUTIFUL GLAMOUR GIRLS

That one really grabbed my attention. Especially when I looked again and read about the live nude models, beautiful ladies wearing nothing but cowboy hats and boots.

I shot a sideways glance at Dad, as if to say, "Remember that good time we had back in Portland? Back at the Star Theater? Why don't we ditch everybody and come back here tonight?"

But Dad just kept going straight ahead, literally walking the straight and narrow path, a disdainful look on his face. He looked like he scorned the whole idea of those disgraceful women parading around in nothing but cowboy hats and boots. Why would anyone with a shred of decency, he seemed to say, want to patronize such a sinful and disgusting sink of depraved corruption? He had a great way of putting on that strait-laced air. He was so intimidating, in fact, with that holier-than-thou routine, that I never had the guts to ask him what a cathouse was.

By the end of the week, we had seen everything at the San Francisco Golden Gate Exhibition. We had seen all of Treasure Island with its lagoons, fountains, plazas, courts, temples and pavilions. It was kind of a relief when we checked out of the motor lodge at Fisherman's Wharf and headed back north to Oregon.

~ * ~

We didn't go back the way we had come. For variety, Dad said we would take Highway 101 along the coast. From the waterfront, we followed Lombard Avenue out through what looked like another park, with endless acres of lawns and trees and red-tiled roofs on stucco buildings. It was the Presidio, Dad said, an Army base set up during the Civil War to defend against enemy warships. It gave the Army a great excuse to build a huge base in the heart of this beautiful city.

We went around a curve and drove onto the Golden Gate Bridge. We had seen this bridge all week from a distance. But now we were finally driving on it, looking up at the high red towers rising up in the morning mists. Looking down from the bridge, it seemed like we were a mile above the water. Dad said both bridges were built about the same time, just a few years earlier. He said the Golden Gate Bridge was a bigger challenge, its towers having to withstand heavy ocean surges and tidal currents. He said it was an engineering wonder of the world.

We crossed the bridge and headed north along Highway 101, past endless green fields, through Santa Rosa, past vineyards and croplands, through town like Cloverdale, Ukiah and Willits, then into the evergreen forests of northern California. We kept going further and further north until the landscape looked more and more like the rain forests of western Oregon. We drove past dozens of little sawmills with stacks of logs and smoking "wigwams" burning sawdust and wood wastes.

As the day wore on, the air turned cold and cloudy. Dad turned on the headlights when a light mist started falling. It looked chillier and chillier outside. Now the trees were redwoods, even bigger than Douglas firs, some of them made into roadside attractions. We stopped to eat at a little café carved right out of a redwood. At another place, Dad actually drove our car through a tunnel cut into a redwood tree. We followed the highway further north and came to a town called Eureka, right on the coast. We kept going north, drove through Crescent City, and later reached the Oregon border.

It almost felt like we were home again. We kept rolling north until we reached the town of Gold Beach, right where the Rogue River spills into the sea. Dad found a motel and we checked in for the night.

Next day, we drove along Highway 101 through Port Orford and Bandon and North Bend, following right along the Pacific coastline to the town of Florence. After lunch, we left the coast and headed east across the Coast Range to Eugene, so Mom could visit dear old Grandma. Then we headed east through Springfield and followed Highway 126 along the McKenzie River to Belknap Springs, up the switchback loops through dense forests to the McKenzie Pass and on through the pine trees to Sisters and back through the sagebrush desert to Redmond.

When we pulled up to our house, Skipper and I jumped out and ran into the yard, glad to be back. We chased each other around for a while, as Dad and our sisters unloaded the suitcases. Mom went to the front door to get the house key from under the doormat. I watched as she pulled the mat back and looked underneath.

"What's this?" she said, as she picked up a playing card. With a sinking heart, I asked to see it. Without a word, she gave it to me and I turned it over. It was the queen of spades.

Seven

Holy crap—the queen of spades! What did it mean? I finally got that Mexican guy off my mind, at least some of the time. Now he comes back again, right to my house! He must've seen the house key—maybe he came inside—maybe he left a booby trap inside to get me! I thought about this day and night. Was he hiding some place, waiting to jump me? He could come out of hiding anytime and zap me for good! It looked hopeless—I was a goner, for sure!

Then one night, Dad came home with some news that gave me some hope. He had "orders from Salem" to transfer to Madras. Madras. I remembered the place we came through when we moved from The Dalles. It wasn't much of a town. But now I loved the place. Maybe now I could get away from that Mexican guy for good. I could hardly wait for moving day.

Once again, we packed cardboard boxes full of dishes and silverware and glasses. We packed sheets and pillows and blankets. Once again, we packed more boxes full of toothpaste, jars of fruit, salt and pepper shakers, canned fruit, photo albums, books, slippers, clothes hangers, hammers, pliers, and every other stupid thing required for a civilized existence.

Then one day, a moving van came to our house. It backed up right over the sidewalk and lawn and shoved its tail end right up to the front step. Two men laid down a wooden bridge from the van to our house. They used hand-trucks to move the refrigerator, piano, sofa, mattresses, box springs and all the other big stuff into the van. They loaded in everything else—tables and chairs, bikes, lamps, throw rugs and all the cardboard boxes full of stuff—then closed the van doors and took off.

Dad fired up the Plymouth and we pulled out, leaving our house on 11th Street in the care of Evelyn. She had a job in Redmond and wanted to stay there for a while. Without much stuff, she was sort of camping out, but that was okay, I guess. We drove the five blocks to downtown, hung a left on Sixth Street, and headed north to Madras. This new town was only about thirty miles away, but it seemed like moving to the other side of the world.

We followed Highway 97 past the tiny village of Terrebonne and crossed on the high bridge over the Crooked River. This was our old Fourth of July place, the bridge where Dad lit firecrackers and threw them over the side, waiting for the first explosion and louder echoes coming off the sheer canyon walls four hundred feet down.

It seemed that all irrigation stopped at the Crooked River. Just beyond the canyon, the landscape was pure desert—sagebrush, bunchgrass and juniper trees—familiar country. We had come through here on the last move. Everyone paid more attention to our surroundings this time. What would it be like living in this little town on the desert floor? Myself, I didn't much care, just so long as that damned Mexican didn't find out where I was.

We kept driving, past an abandoned one-room schoolhouse, and climbed up over a saddle ridge between Juniper Butte and Haystack Butte. Off to our right we could see Grizzly Butte—looking just like a grizzly bear resting on its haunches—and kept going through Culver and Metolius, a village of big dreams with a general store and blocks of empty lots waiting for houses. The highway took us north for several miles, then led us around a hill and sort of sneaked us into Madras.

The highway took a sharp left turn at the business district and headed north through the one-block downtown. We rode a short distance over the dry bed of Willow Creek and past a few old buildings scattered around. We came to a junction where Highway 97 took off toward the northeast and Highway 26 led due north straight up a steep hill to Agency Plains and on to the Warm Springs Indian Reservation.

Dad pulled off to the side of Highway 26 beyond the forks. He looked left and pointed to a house sitting a short distance away on a bench of land within a hillside rising a good distance beyond the house to a rimrock formation framing the top of the hill.

"There's our house," he said. "That's our new home." He crossed the highway, drove up a gravel road and pulled into a driveway alongside the house. We got out and looked around. It sure wasn't Redmond, but Skipper and I decided the place was okay. It looked like a good hideout from the Mexican, and that's all I cared about. The house had three bedrooms and a basement and a big porch under cover and even a little lawn for a touch of green. There was a garage out back for the car, plus an old chicken coop that looked good for a clubhouse. From our viewpoint, we could look south and see the whole town spread out below us.

It wasn't much of a town. The main drag was surrounded by maybe six or seven blocks of houses on both sides, with other houses scattered across the desert floor and south up a hillside. Dad said the population was about five hundred. That didn't seem possible unless they were counting all the cats and dogs.

A short distance away, on the other side of the highway, was the State Highway compound with office, sheds, dump trucks and gravel piles inside a fenced yard next to Willow Creek. This was Dad's command post for maintenance of old highways and construction of some new ones. These included a new forty-mile drive through the Warm Springs Reservation, making it easier for Portland hot-shots to drive over to Madras and central Oregon via Government Camp on Mt. Hood.

In the first weeks after our arrival, Dad took us on weekend jaunts to explore the Jefferson County outback. He took up fossil hunting for a new hobby and he wanted to roam around looking for places to dig. Skipper and I went along just to see what the boondocks looked like. We ate lots of dust. But we saw lots of back country, clear out to Ashwood—said to be an old stagecoach stop—and beyond. Except for some bottomlands, most of it was desert rangeland with sagebrush and bunch grass stretching out in all directions. Sometimes we came across an abandoned homestead with an old weather-beaten house still standing. We always stopped and looked around the place, wondering who lived there, how long they stayed and why they had tried to scratch a living out of this dry and desolate land.

During weekdays, Skipper and I rode our bikes into Madras and explored the town. Unlike Redmond, with irrigation ditches bringing in water for lawns and green trees, Madras was owned by the desert. Each vacant lot was full of sagebrush, and each little breeze sent tumbleweeds rolling down the streets. On the one block of downtown along Highway 97, people angle-parked their cars onto sun-bleached board sidewalks left over from pioneer days. Except for the stone courthouse, a stone bank and a two-story brick building, most buildings were made of wood—one-story hulks built to look magnificent behind second-story facades of wooden false-fronts.

There was something oddly familiar about this place, like I had seen it before in a dream. Then it dawned on me. Take away the cars, and Madras was a frontier town right out of a Gene Autry movie. Madras had it all, except good guys in white hats chasing bad guys in black hats. During those first weeks, we learned more about this little cow town. Even if it looked like a Western movie set, Madras had a good grip on the modern automobile age. Just north of downtown was a Chevrolet dealer, Main Street Motors, with a concrete outpost perched on the south bank of dried-out Willow Creek. Right in the middle of the main drag was Thomas Motors, a Chrysler-Plymouth dealer.

Beautiful downtown Madras was basically one block of buildings on both sides of Highway 97 running north and south through town. On the west side, starting from the north, was an implement company, a hardware store, a tavern called The Club, a barbershop, Jeffway grocery store, and a shoe repair shop. Further south, across the highway, was the two-story Hannon Rooming House. On the east, from the north, was a meat market, the *Madras Pioneer* newspaper office, Pacific Telephone, Thomas Motors, a two-story brick building with a drug store and a clothing store. Further south, across a side street, was the stony fortress of First National Bank next to the Chief Theater.

Across Highway 97 from The Club was the telephone office. Behind a big picture window was a switchboard operated by a lady known as "Central." On the day shift was a tough little blonde woman who was perched on a chair with a pillow high enough so she could reach the switchboard. This particular "Central" mostly ignored those strolling by her window. She kept talking into a headset and connecting what looked like hollow tubes running from one board to another. Sometimes she paused for a moment to look out the window and check out what was going on along the main street. This was an important part of her job. If you were home and wanted to call somebody, you just grabbed the phone and she picked up your signal right away. "Central," you might say, "connect me with Dan Fitzpatrick." She might hook you up to his house without comment. Or she might say, "Dan Fitzpatrick? Forget it. I just saw him going into The Club."

Directly south of Thomas Motors was a two-story brick building owned by Doc Zecchio. On the street level of his building was a drug store. The front window was filled with knee braces, canes, crutches and signs advertising miracle drugs. Next to the window was a door which opened to steps leading up to Doc Zecchio's office on the second floor. Mom took me there once for a cough or a sore throat or something. I was really impressed. He looked a lot more like a real doctor than Doc Jenkins back in Redmond. About medium height, he had gray hair with a professional moustache and a thin nose. He wore a white lab coat, a stethoscope around his neck, and a blood-pressure gauge hanging out of his coat pocket.

His finest touch of authority was a round mirror on his forehead with a little hole in the middle. First thing, he told me to strip to the waist. Then he took my blood pressure and held my tongue down with a wooden stick and looked at my mouth through that hole in the mirror. Then he banged on my back, with his stethoscope on my chest, going "hmmm," which was comforting.

After spending more time messing around like that, he wrote out a prescription, said "goodbye" and disappeared behind a curtain. As we were walking down the front stairs, he must've been hustling down the back steps and changing coats. Going into the drug store, we saw Doc Zecchio was behind the counter dressed in a blue coat. Like a pharmacist. He took our prescription with an air of great curiosity and studied it for a while. Then he went into another room and came back with a bottle full of pills, as prescribed by the doctor upstairs. Mom paid twice, I guess. What an onta-pra-newer!

Near the courthouse was a little cafe with just enough seats to handle a bus-load of people. Around noon, the Trailways bus pulled in from Portland and hissed to a stop. The passengers got off and stretched and looked around and filed inside for a half-hour stop. The café had a good smell of steaming coffee and hamburgers sizzling on the grill. It buzzed with the happy sounds of people finding relief and good food on their way south. I thought maybe Madras should've been named Pit Stop.

A month after we arrived, the school district had a notice in the local paper. They were going to hold a picnic at Cove Palisades State Park, down in the bottom of Crooked River canyon, to celebrate the beginning of another school year. Dad and Mom decided we should attend this picnic to meet the locals. So, the next Saturday morning, we loaded up the car with food and picnic supplies and took off.

To get there, we followed Highway 97 back toward Culver, then hung a right and followed a paved county road due west. In a few miles, we came to the edge of a canyon maybe a thousand feet deep. It was the same Crooked River we crossed on the high bridge near Terrebonne. But here the canyon was wider and much deeper and it had walls sloping down just enough to carve out a narrow gravel road down to the bottom.

With my heart in my throat, I watched Dad wheel our car down into the canyon along the narrow road. He slowed to a crawl and eased our way along—especially on hairpin turns—and I was praying nobody was coming up from below. I could imagine us going over the side and rolling over a million times before hitting the bottom. Nothing like that happened and Dad acted like it was no big deal. Eventually we worked our way down to the bottom of the canyon and drove past a sign reading "Cove Palisades State Park." When we pulled up and parked, I was amazed at how many other families had driven into that deep canyon. It was a different world down there, away from the desert, with the smell of grass and water in the air. We were right next to the Crooked River, rattling over the rocks as it rushed to meet the Deschutes River a mile downstream. The park was huge, with lawns and softball diamonds, a community kitchen under roof and lots of picnic tables all over the place.

We got out of the car and looked over the crowd of kids and grownups milling around and talking. Mom waded right into the crowd, introducing herself and getting acquainted. I was watching all this when my eyes fell on the cutest little girl I had ever seen. She was about my age, with nice soft eyes, a lovely face and dark brown hair which came half-way down her back. She looked like the movie star Linda Darnell, wearing jeans and a denim shirt. She was gorgeous. I couldn't take my eyes off her. But I didn't have enough guts to walk up and say hello.

After a while, somebody organized a game of rotation softball. I started out in left field and worked my way around the bases. Just two spots ahead of me was Miss Linda Darnell, catching and throwing the softball quite well. I was watching her so much, I almost missed a couple of easy catches myself. Finally, I worked my way to the pitcher's mound and it was my turn to pitch. I wanted to show off and strike out the batter with three blazing pitches. But then I realized that my batter was the cute girl with the long brown hair.

Right away, I gave up the idea of being a big hero. I wanted to make points with her, if possible. Only way for me was to help her get on first base. So I pretended to wind up real good and then let go with a real creampuff soft pitch. It was too soft, I guess, 'cause she took a hard swing and missed. So I wound up and threw another slow pitch. She swung hard and missed again. Now I was in real trouble. She stood in the batter's box, looking like she wanted to really nail my last pitch and send the ball clear out in the river. I tossed my last pitch, slow as I could make it, right over the plate. She took a mighty swing and missed! Not even a foul ball. She just struck out. And I was the stupid sap who had thrown the pitches. Now I would be her enemy for life. I wanted to haul back and kick myself in the ass, I was so pissed-off at myself. She dropped the bat and ran back to the outfield as I watched her run away from my life for good.

Then somebody called off the game because it was time to eat. I walked over to our picnic table where Mom had laid out a tablecloth covered with lunch goodies. I was standing there, when a guy came up alongside me.

"How come you struck Beverly out?" he said.

"I tried to let her hit!" I yelled. "I gave her the slowest pitch I could!"

He laughed in a hearty way and patted me on the shoulder. "Just kidding," he said. I looked him over. He was about a year older than me and heavier. He had thick black hair, combed straight back, with a tanned face and a big smile.

"My name is Todd," he said. "Todd McKinney. And over there," he added, pointing to the lovely girl I had struck out, "is Beverly Nelson. She lives twenty miles north of town. On a ranch along Trout Creek."

Boy, was this guy a fountain of information! "Sit down and have some lunch," I said, grabbing him before he could get away. He sat without any argument. I introduced him to Mom and Dad and Skipper. Then I gave him every-thing I had to offer. I popped open a Coke bottle for him and filled his plate with fried chicken and potato salad and baked beans. He happily downed all this food, smiling and asking questions.

"Where did you move here from?" and "How many in your family?" and "Where in Madras do you live?" and "What kind of business you in?"

I could see why this Todd McKinney knew so much. He made it his business to know everything about everybody. But so what? What did it matter? He could tell me everything I needed to know about this fabulous girl in the jeans and denim shirt. I dished out a big scoop of ice cream for him. He dug in with a big smile, telling us all about the ranch where he lived out on Hay Creek. I looked around for the girl—Beverly, was that her name?—but didn't see her. McKinney watched me craning my neck. He got up from the table and touched my shoulder as he walked away. I jumped up and walked with him back toward the outdoor kitchen. "Beverly had to go home early with her family," he said. "They had some kind of problem with one of their horses."

I really had to admire this guy, Mr. Information, who had the goods on everybody. As he walked away, he turned and smiled in a way that said we were buddies. I hoped it was true.

~ * ~

Back home in Madras, Skipper and I kept looking for new ways to explore. One day we followed a gravel road running past our house and straight up the hill. We walked the road to its end, beyond an old barn and farmhouse, and kept climbing up through the sagebrush to the base of the rimrock. We hiked along the rock base and found a gap, then climbed up through the formation and finally reached the top. We came up on a broad plateau, flat as a table. It was Agency Plains we had heard about. We walked away from the rimrock a short way and came to a double set of heavy-duty railroad tracks. This was the mainline railroad running from the Columbia River to Bend and beyond to California. As we walked along the tracks, I saw a circle painted on a railroad tie with an arrow and some strange writing.

"Look at this!" I said to Skipper. "Look at this sign!"

"What's it mean?"

"Search me! It's secret hobo writing, I guess."

We lay on the tracks to get a better look. The writing around the circle made no sense at all. It had all kinds of little jiggles and notches.

"Look!" I said. "That arrow points straight to our house!"

"Sure does! It creeps me out!"

"Me, too. I think it's 'cause Mom gave that hobo a good meal."

Right after we had moved to Madras, a hobo came by our house. He was dirty and his face was all whiskery and he smelled bad. He showed up when Mom was hanging out some laundry to dry. He said he was hungry and asked to work for some food.

Mom took pity on him, I guess, and told him to chop some firewood for the cast-iron stove in the kitchen. He took the axe and started chopping wood like crazy, almost like he enjoyed it, chopping more wood than Mom needed. Finally, she motioned him to quit, go inside and sit down. Then she cooked him a hot meal with meat and potatoes and some carrots, maybe the best meal he'd had in a long time. When he was finished, he thanked her over and over before he walked away, stopping and waving before turning and walking back up the hill toward the rimrock. We all felt good about giving the guy a meal. But I didn't like finding thi hobo sign pointing straight to our house. We tried to mess it up, but it was carved into the railroad tie and couldn't be taken out. So we tried to forget about it. I had enough worries, like that Mexican, and didn't need any more.

Veronica really liked popular music and she liked to keep track of the top hits. She did this by listening to the Bend radio station, especially on Saturday nights, with a radio show called *Your Hit Parade*. But she often had a date on Saturday night. That's when I got stuck with catching the program and keeping track of how the songs ranked that week, including my two favorites, "Pennsylvania 6-5000" and "Chattanooga Choo-Choo."

Now and then, Mom and Dad would visit some friends in town for an evening of bridge. They usually had Veronica baby-sit us, but sometimes she had a date and wasn't available. That happened one Saturday night when all their social calendars were filled up. They had a big discussion and decided I was old enough to watch over the house and take care of Skipper.

It was a nasty evening, with a heavy desert rainstorm and bursts of wind rattling the windows. After they left for the evening, I sat listening to the radio—trying to keep track of that week's top tunes—when I heard some pounding on the front door. It was dark outside, so I turned on the porch light. Standing there was a big guy with bloodshot eyes and scraggly old beard, wearing a shabby black coat that he clutched around himself. He was unsteady on his feet and swayed as the wind seemed to blow him sideways.

"Got any wine?" he shouted through the window in the front door.

"No!" I yelled back, shaking my head.

"I'll give ya a dollar if ya let me in!"

"No!" I yelled back. "Get outta here or I'll call the cops!"

That did the trick. He turned and staggered down the steps to the ground and disappeared into the night. That's all there was to it. But when Mom and Dad got home that night and I told them about it, it scared the heck out of them. They praised me over and over for the way I handled it. All said and done, that evening gave me a bunch of brownie points for the next time I got in trouble. And I think it got Mom worked up enough to start hammering on Dad to move out of the "country" and into a house right in town.

~ * ~

During that year of 1940, the war was really heating up in Europe. France had surrendered to Hitler. England was getting bombed by the German Luftwaffe, and the Royal Air Force was fighting back. The Battle of Britain was going on full blast. In quiet little Madras, all that seemed to be happening on another planet. But war fever was slowly gathering steam, even in our little corner of the country. One day in August, we were surprised to see a parade of Army trucks full of troops heading north. It went on for an hour—an endless convoy of olive-drab jeeps and trucks pulling cannons—stretching as far as we could see, from the south where they came into view to Lyle Gap several miles north of town. Finally, the convoy was gone and everybody went back to their normal routines. It was obvious that our country was getting ready to join the big fight overseas.

~ * ~

In September, I entered the seventh grade at Madras Grade School. It was fun to see the kids I had met earlier. Especially the lovely Beverly Nelson.

My new buddy, Todd McKinney, rode to school with her and four other kids every day in a station wagon from the ranch country. On the first day, I was standing by the curb when they pulled up and stopped. I just stood there and gawked as they all piled out and walked into the school.

This grade school was set up differently than Redmond, where each grade had its own room and designated teacher. In Madras, they mixed two or three grades together. McKinney said that was better than the one-room school concept, where he started in first grade. He said they had just one classroom with one teacher. All the grades, first to eighth, got the same stuff together at the same time.

In Madras, we had three teachers. The first and second grades were taught by Miss Green. The third, fourth, and fifth grades had Miss Robertson. The sixth, seventh, and eighth grades were taught by Mr. Sterling Baxter, the principal.

Mr. Baxter wasn't a bad-looking dude for an old guy. I mean, he didn't have any big bumps on his nose and he wasn't cross-eyed and his teeth weren't all yellow and his ears didn't stick out like jug handles. He had all his hair, which was thick and black and parted on the left side. He was a smoothie, in fact, but he did like to talk a lot. Maybe too much. He gave us a lecture each day on books he had read, people he had known, mistakes he had made, lessons he had learned from tricky situations, good stuff about real life.

When he talked, he looked left and then right—like he was giving an important address—but we didn't have to jump up and clap every minute. If somebody asked him anything out of left field, he puckered his lips as if to say "that was a stupid question," so most of us had sense enough to keep our mouths shut.

In Mr. Baxter's class, we had the usual lessons in arithmetic, writing, reading, geography, and history. But those lectures of his were fun because they gave us lots of stuff to think about. Like how much things really cost. And he gave us lots of war news—probably stuff he read in the paper—about the Battle of Britain going on, England's Royal Air Force standing alone against Nazi Germany.

I cared about the Battle of Britain. It was exciting, sure, to hear about those Spitfires having dogfights with the Luftwaffe planes. But most of the time my mind was on Beverly Nelson. During that first week of school, I finally had the guts to talk with her one day during recess.

"Do you like playing softball?" I asked.

"I did until you struck me out." Then she laughed and put her hand on my arm. "Just kidding. You gave me some easy pitches. I just couldn't hit anything."

"Then you're not mad at me?"

"Of course not."

"Wow, that's great!" I wanted to run and jump and turn handsprings. Except I didn't know how to do any stupid handsprings.

"Will you be my girlfriend?"

"Maybe," she replied, with a shy glance. "Now, I have to go play on the teeter-totter. I promised Todd." She ran over to where McKinney was waiting. She climbed up on the teeter-totter with an easy grace and started bouncing the thing up and down. I felt giddy and excited that I wanted to do something crazy. Good thing the school bell rang before I could think of anything.

Back in the classroom, she sat about three rows ahead of me and off to the left. I couldn't take my eyes off her. I had to do something to show how I felt about her. I took my square eraser and wrote both our names on it. Then I connected the names with a line and a heart in the middle and a line of xxxxxxxxxxxx, meaning kisses. I worked on it during another Battle of Britain lecture by Mr. Baxter. I worked so hard, he probably thought I was taking notes on his profound thoughts. Later, I gave the eraser to Beverly. She looked at it with a little smile and put it in her jacket. She kept it—I couldn't believe my luck!

Eight

It seems Jefferson County was the last follower of old pioneer customs, making Madras a sort of cow town Brigadoon. One example was the 'box social', held to raise money for some worthy cause. About a month into the school year, the school board held a box social at Madras High School. All the parents and kids were expected to attend. This included the Nelson family, who came in from their ranch on Trout Creek.

The way it worked, older grade school girls and high school girls were asked to bring a picnic lunch for two in a box wrapped up like a birthday present. Each girl "secretly" told her boyfriend what her lunch box looked like. He in turn was expected to outbid any rivals for the joy of sharing the picnic lunch with her.

Naturally, no boyfriend—or would-be boyfriend—could allow anyone to outbid him. Naturally, this made all kinds of money for those who organized the box social. To my delight, Beverly told me she had brought a blue box with a red ribbon and bow. I found the box right away in the pile of other boxes. When it came up for auction,

I started out as the only bidder. Then—just my luck—Mark Collins started bidding against me. He had figured out what was going on and wanted to be the lucky guy to sit with her.

Mark Collins was a kid I knew in school, but one I didn't like much. He was about my height and weight, but seemed bigger and stronger. He had a large jaw, curly brown hair and eyes that looked like he was pissed-off about something all the time. He frowned a lot, but if he smiled, his lips curled into a kind of sneer. He was very competitive, always wanting to race you over to the next block or challenging you to jump higher than he could. Stuff like that. I never thought he had the same feelings I did. About Beverly Nelson, I mean.

So I would never have put that rotten Mark Collins on any kind of rivals list. Yet, there he was, bidding against me for the fun of sharing a picnic lunch with Beverly Nelson. By the time it was over, I had borrowed a bunch of money from Mom. But it was worth it. Beverly and I took her blue box over to a corner of the gym. We sat, side by side, on some folding chairs lined up along the wall. We opened the box and took out the goodies she had prepared and ate them in silence. Just like a real date. Boy, I thought, this is great!

The next day, Collins came up to me at recess.

"So you beat me at the box social?" he said.

"What's that, a question? You know darn well I beat you."

He kinda laughed in that smirking way of his.

"I know you won. And I know you had to borrow lots of money, too."

"So what? It was worth every penny. Wanna fight about it?" He snickered again.

"Hey, take it easy. I don't want to fight you. I want to show you how to make enough money to pay it back."

"Oh, yeah? How's that?"

"Collecting beer bottles along the highway."

He came up with a good idea, I'll give him that. Every weekend, we rode our bikes south along Highway 97 picking up beer bottles on each side of the road. Other times we followed the highway north of town for a few miles to pick up the bottles. We had baskets on our bikes to carry them and usually came back with a big pile. I got the owner of The Club to give us some empty cases. We filled them with the bottles and stacked them in the alley behind The Club.

But we worried that somebody might steal our valuable goods, so we built a little warehouse a block north of downtown out in some sagebrush flats. We built it along an unofficial dirt road wandering between two wooden sheds used for storing heavy machinery. Behind one shed, we found several pieces of plywood and wooden bracing from machinery packing cases. We hammered them together and made a little warehouse to keep our cases of bottles stacked up and out of sight. A tavern guy helped me contact the people who delivered the beer each week.

The next Thursday afternoon, right after school, we rode our bikes down to our warehouse. Right on schedule, a big truck and trailer from Bend Distributing Company pulled into our little private road and stopped at our warehouse. The driver loaded up our cases of bottles and wrote out an invoice. Collins and I looked it over and agreed on the number of cases and signed the invoice. Then the driver gave us cash for the bottles, which we split fifty-fifty. Now we were really in business! Ontra-pra-newers! Awesome!

After that, on the first Thursday of each month at four o'clock, that big old eighteen-wheeler came up our road and stopped at our little warehouse. Each time, the driver loaded up the bottles and wrote out an invoice which we signed. Each time, the driver gave us a wad of cash which we split. Boy, what fun! Just like I thought all along, being an onta-pra-newer was the absolute greatest thing in the whole wide world!

One Thursday, the Bend Distributing guy counted our cases and gave us an invoice to sign, as usual, and handed over seven dollars and forty cents. We shook hands with him and watched as he climbed back into his tractor-trailer rig and slowly followed our little dirt road through the sagebrush back to the city streets.

Collins turned to me. "I should get most of this money," he said. "I picked up most of the bottles." I laughed a little and shook my head.

"No way. This is a fifty-fifty partnership. I don't care how many bottles you picked up. We split fifty-fifty. That's the deal we made."

I leaned over to stack some empty beer cases. Then it came—WHAM!—a sucker shot to my right ear. I staggered a little, but came back at him—BAM!— with a shot to his face that started a nosebleed. We stood there and traded blows—BAM!—WHAM!—but neither went down. Then we both just stopped and looked at each other. Collins pulled out a handkerchief and wiped his nose. Then he turned and walked away. It was all over. We never spoke about it again.

~ * ~

Several times, Todd McKinney invited me out to his ranch for a weekend. We hiked all over the place, shooting at jackrabbits and crows with his .22 rifle. Sometimes we rode horseback. Old McKinney was very patient in teaching me and I learned to enjoy riding out over the hills and far-flung fields of his family ranch.

Back at the ranch headquarters, we slept in a bunkhouse a good walk away from the main house. One Saturday morning, I was shaken awake by McKinney before dawn and had to dress fast in the ice-cold room. There was a tiny sliver of light in the eastern sky as we walked through the frosty grass to the house. Inside, we entered a world of warmth and good smells of food cooking and the happy sounds of people talking and laughing around a huge table just off the kitchen. At the head sat Todd's father, Arch McKinney, holding court and giving orders for the day like a Scottish chieftain. The table was loaded with piles of steaming eggs, fried potatoes, bacon and pancakes. It was delicious, maybe more so because of the friendly banter at the table.

As McKinney showed me the rest of the house, I was fascinated by one room in particular. The entry was barred by a velvet rope and all the furniture inside covered with sheets. He said that room was the parlor, used only for high social occasions. Probably another old pioneer custom.

At McKinney's place, I discovered the ranchers had different phones than in Madras. His phone was a big old wooden box, thick and wide and about three feet tall. It was so heavy it had to be mounted on the wall studs. This big box had a crank on the side to send a signal, an earpiece at the end of a long cord, and a black mouthpiece in the front to yell into once you got somebody on the line. To call another rancher, you cranked their signal—say, two longs and a short—and the person who heard his signal ring would pick up the earpiece and yell "hello" into the mouthpiece to start the talk. That was okay. But it was a party line, so everybody else could pick up their earpiece to listen in. And everybody else usually did. A few years back, it was said, a college boy from Bend called his sweetheart on the party line to propose marriage. When she hesitated for a second, several voices quickly broke in urging her to accept.

One weekend I was visiting McKinney when he suggested riding to the base of a hill and hiking up to an old Indian cave to look for some arrowheads. That sounded like fun to me, so we saddled up a couple of horses and rode along the county road toward a place we could leave the horses before climbing the hill. We were late getting started and McKinney was worried about running out of time.

We stopped at a gate. He got off and swung it open and I rode through. "We'll take this shortcut," he said. "They shouldn't mind us cutting across the field here." He led his horse through, closed the gate, and climbed back on. We walked the horses across an alfalfa field toward a rocky hillside.

Then we saw a horseman riding toward us at full gallop. We watched as he drew closer and finally thundered up to a stop. He was an old guy with a walrus moustache, slit eyes and a face of wrinkled rawhide under a big slouch hat. He wore a black leather vest over a white shirt, with dirty old jeans and the meanest pair of six-guns you ever saw.

"What're you punks doing on my land?" he yelled. We hadn't studied Rhetorical Questions yet, but I knew enough to keep my big mouth shut. "Ya got one minute to get off my place! Or I'll drop the both of ya!"

McKinney wheeled his horse around and kicked him and took off. I did the same. We flew across the field, hooves kicking up dirt and alfalfa. I leaned down over the sharp ridge of my horse's neck, face buried in the flying mane, afraid the old man might open fire. In no time at all, we bounced up to the gate. Todd jumped off and swung it open and I trotted through. Then he came through, closed the gate, remounted and we walked our horses along the road. For a while we were silent.

"He looks like a ghost from the Old West," I said at last.

"He's no ghost. But, yeah, he's from the Old West. He was born during the Civil War."

"How come you know so much about him?"

"That was Dan Riggs. That was my grandfather. He just doesn't know me anymore."

McKinney learned how to run a tractor when he was eleven and he learned how to drive a car not long after. So, it was only natural he would borrow the family car sometimes and drive someplace. That was probably against all the Oregon laws, but enforcement was pretty relaxed. The general rule seemed to be that any farm kid who drove a tractor could drive a car any place he wanted to go, even on a state highway.

One time he said we would drive over to the Nelson ranch for a visit. I got into the car and watched in wonder as he casually drove down the county road and followed it to Highway 97. We took the highway north past the Willowdale store and turned off onto a gravel road. Driving across a cattle guard, we entered a scene right out of a calendar. To our right was a large hip-roof barn. On our left ran the bubbling waters of Trout Creek. Beyond that was a big two-story house with gables and chimneys and a big front porch. The house was framed by a grove of poplar trees, giving it a serene and sheltered look.

"Beverly's great-grandfather homesteaded this place back in the 1870s," Todd said. "He ran a stagecoach stop here. He also had a contract to keep the stage road open from Trout Creek to Antelope and Shaniko and clear over to Bakeoven."

We spent a couple of hours there, visiting with Beverly and her mother. Nothing much happened, just lots of talk. To McKinney, this was no big deal. But to me, it was awesome. When Beverly and her mother served us some hot chocolate and cookies, it's a miracle I didn't spill everything on the rug in my excitement. While McKinney was giving out the latest gossip, I just sat and dreamed about Beverly and me riding horses together somewhere on the ranch. I could just see us stopping someplace, tying up the horses, then lying down on the grass together. I had no idea what would happen after that, but it fired me up just thinking about the possibilities.

~ * ~

Back in Madras, an Army convoy came through about every other month. Hundreds of olive-drab trucks with big white stars on the sides, going north, with soldiers riding in the back. On and on they came, soldiers driving jeeps, command cars and still more trucks full of soldiers. An endless parade heading north on Highway 97, a steady stream visible from two miles south of town to Lyle Gap on the north. All the trucks, always heading north. What was going on? Were they planning on a war with Canada?

~ * ~

One day, I heard that Main Street Motors was sponsoring a Soap Box Derby open to all kids in Jefferson County. I always had some notion about building a downhill racing car. This gave me a good excuse. So I biked over to the Chevrolet dealer and filled out an entry form. As I found out, Mark Collins was the first one to enter the race. I could just imagine his reaction when he found out I entered, too. I could see him going "Yeah!" and pumping his stupid fist when he found out. This deal was right down his alley. He loved competition and I knew he wanted to beat me in this Soap Box Derby more than anything else in the world.

About a mile out of town was a little junkyard with some rusty old cars sitting around. I rode out there on my bike and bought a steering wheel and some other stuff that might come in handy. Back home, I took the four tires off a wagon we had. I found some lumber and started building the car. I didn't have any plans drawn up, just a fairly good idea of what I was trying to get done.

With lots of sawing and hammering, I put together a platform about two feet wide by eight feet long, which came to a point at each end. For stability and turning radius, I mounted the wheels on two-by-four out-riggers sticking out about two feet on each side. To turn the car, I bolted the center of the front outrigger to the car, then rigged up a device with ropes attached to the steering column. For brakes, I bolted a one-by-two piece on the right side—pulling back on the handle would drag it on the ground—and nailed on some old tire tread where the wood meets the road. I built a frame of one-by-twos to enclose my legs and another frame to support my back. I built a seat of plywood and used some old car upholstery to make the seat and back cushions. I covered both frames by nailing on sheet aluminum from an old sign. Finally, I painted the aluminum with some bright red paint for a racy look.

During this time, Collins came up to my house once to talk about the race in a friendly way. What he was really doing was spying on the enemy. He never said how his car was coming along and I didn't ask him. I knew how badly he wanted to win the race. But I still underestimated just how important this race was to him. He was a tough kid, very competitive. But I never imagined how far he would go to win.

As race day drew near, it became clear the Soap Box Derby had boiled down to a contest between Mark Collins and me. Period. The reason was simple—no other kids in Jefferson County had bothered to build a racing car. With a valiant effort to save face all around, Main Street Motors played it up big. They made it sound like this race would rival the Indianapolis 500. They strung up banners all over the place and ran ads and stories in the Madras *Pioneer* inviting all to come out for the Big Race on Saturday morning.

In any other town, a Soap Box Derby would be run on a gentle little slope with stripes keeping each car in its proper lane and with officials everywhere to make sure everything was done according to strict rules. In Madras, however, it was the first—and last—Soap Box Derby they ever held. To beef up the excitement, they decided to run the race down Highway 26 from Agency Plains to Madras. This was over a mile long and down a steep grade. How they got the state highway closed for an hour is a mystery. It must've taken some real political arm-twisting over in Salem, and I'm sure Dad didn't touch this thing with a twenty-foot pole.

At 9:30 on Saturday morning, the Main Street Motors guys loaded me and Collins, along with our little cars, onto the back of a truck. They drove us up to the top of the hill. Then they unloaded our cars and lined them up—Collins' car on the left side and my car on the right side of the yellow line. Then, after standing around for a while, we climbed into our cars and waited. Nobody warned us to stay on our side of the highway. They just assumed each one of us would stay in his own lane.

As we sat there waiting, I could see the crowd strung out across the highway down at the bottom of the hill. The race officials talked for a while and one of them got behind each car. Then someone shot off a pistol and they pushed our cars to get us going. In no time, I was shooting down the highway, going faster than I ever dreamed of going. At first, Collins and I were running neck-and-neck and then I gained about a car length on him. But I wasn't thinking about the race so much as wondering if my car would hold together long enough to make it all the way down to the bottom of the hill.

Then it happened. Collins crossed the yellow line and came straight at me—he ran his car right into the side of my car! He was trying to run me off the road! I couldn't believe it—Collins, my old business partner, was trying to run me off the road! Then I got mad and yanked my steering wheel around. If he wants to play bumper cars, okay, we play bumper cars. I steered my car at his car and tried to ram *his* car and run *him* off the road. And that's where my outrigger wheels came in handy—they had more reach and leverage than his wheels—and they locked around the front of his car. We went roaring down the hill together— the front end of my car just ahead of his car as we came screaming across the finish line—so I won the race. But those spectators strung out across the highway were right in front of us, just twenty yards beyond the finish line. I yanked back on my brake hard as I could, trying to stop both cars, and by some miracle we came skidding to a stop just before we would have slammed right into the crowd.

They cleared the people off the highway, pushed our cars over to the side and opened up the highway to regular cars again. As people left to go home, several came over to talk about the race. Collins didn't say a word. He just untangled his car from mine and pushed it along the road toward his house. He had failed big-time, in his eyes, not winning the race. And his crazy plan to run me off the road hadn't worked as expected, even though he loaded up his car's insides with bricks to make a better battering ram.

As I stood and watched him, I felt an arm draped around my shoulder. Smiling at this friendly gesture, I turned and saw—the Mexican!

"What do you want?" I yelled in his face.

He said nothing. His face gave no clue—a zero expression. But he handed me a card. I turned it over. It was the king of spades!

When I looked up again, he was gone. Disappeared into the crowd. I had almost forgotten about him. I thought he would never find me here in Madras. How did he find me? What did it mean? What did he want?

Soon after that, Mom said we had rented a house in downtown Madras, just one block from downtown. Another move. Only this time I knew I couldn't escape from the Mexican. What about those cards? All of them in spades. What did that mean? Some kind of disaster? Some kind of danger? *He's still out there,* I thought. He found out I live in this little town of Madras. He's set to grab me or stab me, whenever the time is right. It could happen any day, at any time!

I threw myself into the move, trying to take my mind off that damned Mexican. Once again, we packed all the little stuff in cardboard boxes. Once again, a moving van came with two guys to load up all the big stuff and take it to our new house downtown. I went through the motions like a zombie, thinking and thinking about the Mexican. How did he find me? What does he want? What's he gonna do to me?

When we moved into the new house in town, it seemed more complicated than before. Because it was so close to the old house, there was no need to take everything in one trip. So we made a million trips before we finally got all the stuff moved down off the hill and into our new place in town. I didn't mind all this extra work and effort since it gave me something else to think about. For a while, anyway.

In a big vacant area behind our new house, Skipper and I found a pit dug in the ground. It was a couple feet deep and maybe twenty feet across. About thirty years earlier, we found out, the Union Pacific and Great Northern each tried to build a railroad south from the Columbia River to California, going along opposite sides of the Deschutes River canyon. This race turned into a real war between the companies—road gangs shooting at each other and blowing up supplies and equipment, the workers sometimes slugging it out with axe handles. By the time they laid tracks almost to Madras in 1911, the Governor figured the war had gone on long enough. He made the two companies merge into one railroad called the Oregon Trunk. They used the best parts of each line—grades, bridges, tunnels—and just left all the other stuff to the jackrabbits. Soon after that, the town held a big party to celebrate the truce and salute the arrival of the railroad.

That hole in our back yard was the remains of a barbeque pit dug out when they held the party. I got this from an old veterinarian named Pete Taylor who had lived around there forever. He said they had a parade with a brass band and lots of guys on horseback and a crowd of maybe six thousand people who came for the parade and barbeque. He said they cooked a whole steer in the pit along with potatoes and beans and salad and tons of coffee for the folks who came to soak up the atmosphere and hear speeches by the railroad men.

Thirty years later, that old barbeque pit was still there, ready for another party in case something big happened. As we found out, things don't change much by themselves in the desert.

Nine

Hitler's panzer divisions, using "blitzkrieg" tactics, advanced deep into Russia. The Second World War was picking up steam. I sure didn't need Mr. Baxter to keep me posted on that. It was big news in all the papers and Dad talked about it a lot. Sooner or later, he said, America would get sucked into the mess.

In Madras, this was made apparent by more Army truck convoys coming through, always heading north. Once a convoy stopped and set up an overnight bivouac in a vacant field just outside town. The USO—United Service Organization—took over the community hall for a dance. The soldiers—nobody called them G.I.s yet—wore uniforms of the First World War. Their helmets were round on top with a flat rim just above the ears. Dress uniforms were khaki shirts and olive-drab wool jackets with baggy woolen pants tucked into high-laced boots. White leggings covered the upper boots—Iike gaiters worn by mountain climbers—maybe just for looks. The community hall had a juke-box with Glenn Miller and Tommy Dorsey records. Lots of ladies from miles around showed up to go dancing with the soldiers. Next day, the Army folded up its tents, loaded up its troops and headed north again.

~ * ~

Our new house had one big advantage. It was only a block from the Chief Theater, so it was lots easier to take in a movie. One we saw was *Down Argentine Way* with Betty Grable as a New York debutante and Don Ameche as the phony son of an Argentine rancher who breeds horses for jumping. There's bad blood between the fathers, which gives the movie something besides Ameche strutting around in gaucho outfits. The best part was Grable singing and dancing at parties. Movies like that helped take my mind off that Mexican guy, at least for a while.

Mom had something to worry about, too. She never stopped worrying that I might turn out like Uncle Erik. She was always looking for some "character-building" experience to give me a stupid work ethic.

By this time, the economy had recovered somewhat. The war overseas had lifted crop prices, so farmers were in good shape again. Their only problem was, ranch hands were in short supply. Lots of men had left the farms to find good jobs in the cities.

One day in church, Mom got to talking with a Mr. Vanderveer, who owned a couple sections of wheat land up on Agency Plains. When he complained about how tough it was to find good help for the wheat harvest, Mom had a divine inspiration. She offered my services for the duration of the wheat harvest. He accepted and the stupid deal was done. Another Grownup Attack, with Mom leading the charge!

When she gave me the news, she smiled with a serene kind of self-assurance about the wisdom of this move. She said it would be a good "character-building" experience for me. And so, on a lovely Sunday evening in the midst of a beautiful summer, Mr. Vanderveer was scheduled to arrive at our home to collect his newest half-assed hired hand. With a shivering dread of the unknown, I had packed my gym bag with underwear and socks, comb and toothbrush, extra shirt, and baseball hat. I had put on my hiking boots and rolled up my sleeping bag and thrown in some leather gloves.

There was a knock at the door. It was like a knock from Hell and it sent a shudder through my little twelve-year-old body.

When Mom opened the door, Mr. Vanderveer was standing there in bib overalls and plaid shirt. He was a stocky man, with a large head and thick-lipped mouth and he smiled at me like an executioner sizing up his next victim. He said hello to Mom, shook my hand and said I would do just fine as a ranch hand. I said goodbye to Dad, Mom and Skipper, feeling like I was going away forever. Carrying my crummy gym bag and sleeping bag, I followed Mr. Vanderveer to his pickup for the drive out to his ranch.

I just hoped I would be paid something for all this misery, but nobody said if I would get paid or how much it would be. Later I found out my pay was two dollars and fifty cents a day. Working twelve hours each day, my grade school math told me I would be making about twenty cents an hour.

We followed Highway 26 up the hill to Agency Plains—the same highway I had gone down in the Soap Box Derby a million years ago—and drove west on the highway for several miles. Then Mr. Vanderveer took a right turn and drove along a paved county road and turned onto a gravel road running alongside endless fields of wheat. Finally, he pulled off the road and steered the pickup into his place. He drove past some shabby wooden buildings and parked under a windbreak of poplar trees. I could see this place was all business—even the trees had a job—which made me feel even more miserable. The only good thing was, I could forget all my worrying about the Mexican for a while.

The ranch headquarters featured an old two-storied farmhouse in a pocket of packed dirt and weeds, surrounded by wheat fields on all sides. Tractors, plows and other farm implements were parked here and there between a small barn and bunkhouse, near a low-slung cabin which turned out to be the cookhouse.

"We have breakfast from five to six in the morning," said Mr. Vanderveer, "before going to work in the fields. There's the bunkhouse over there. Go over there and find yourself a bed and get some sleep."

The reality of this place hit me like a bucket of hog slop. Like a zombie, I walked across a gravel road and up to the bunkhouse. I opened the door and went inside. It was a cruddy little shack of several rooms and a toilet down the hall. The only room left had a rusty bed frame and springs, with a stained and sagging mattress covered by a dirty old blanket. I opened the closet door—CRASH!—as empty whiskey bottles spilled out and clattered across the floor. Like the Fibber McGee show, only not so funny this time.

With a sigh, I laid out my sleeping bag on the blanket and tried to fluff up a soiled old pillow sitting there. It was starting to get kinda dark, so I thought I should try to get some sleep. I stripped to my underwear and climbed in the sleeping bag and stared up at the smoke-stained ceiling. I had never felt so lonesome and so desolate before. For the first time in my life, I was homesick. This job was going to be like a jail sentence, I told myself, but it had to end sometime. Eventually, I would serve my time. Sooner or later, they had to let me out of this stupid place. Eventually, they had to let me go home. In the meantime, I just had to live through it. I lay there for a long time, thinking about that, listening to the pack-rats scratching around in the attic above, and finally went to sleep.

Early next morning, I woke to the sounds of my bunkhouse cellmates —hacking and coughing and spitting—and the smell of cigarette smoke wafting through the halls. I looked at my watch. It was about 4:30. I jumped out of bed, pulled on my clothes, laced up my boots and went outside. It was still dark but the sun was threatening to break over the horizon. I could see it was going to be a great day. A great day for going on a picnic at Suttle Lake or fishing at East Lake. But not me. No, I was going to spend this great day harvesting wheat. And the day after that and the next day and the next day, forever and ever. I had no idea what kind of lousy work I would be doing in this wheat harvest. But I knew I would be finding out real soon.

Just then came a loud clanging noise from the cookhouse. I looked and saw a plump woman with black hair tied up with a red bandana banging on an iron triangle hanging from the ceiling of the porch. Nobody told me, but I guessed that was the call to breakfast. Especially when I saw the other hired hands rushing over there. I followed them inside and saw a large picnic table loaded with potatoes, fried eggs, bacon and sausage and pots of coffee waiting to be poured. My cellmates were a rough-looking bunch. Bleary-eyed and unshaven, they looked like escaped convicts from the State Pen. One guy moved over to make room for me. I slid in next to him and helped myself to the food. No one said "hello" or anything. There was no easy banter like at Todd McKinney's place. Each guy was too busy shoveling food in his mouth. There was no talk except "pass the salt," or "pass the biscuit" or "pass the coffee."

About the time we finished eating, Mr. Vanderveer came in and said it was time to go to work. I got up and followed the other guys outside. They climbed up on the back end of a pickup, so I climbed up there, too. We shared the space with two big fuel barrels jammed up against the pickup cabin.

Mr. Vanderveer fired up the truck and drove us a couple miles to a wheat field. He drove out on the field and pulled up alongside a combine hooked up to a Caterpillar tractor. Everybody jumped out so I jumped out, too.

They pumped diesel fuel from one barrel into the Cat and gas from the other barrel into the combine. The "Cat-skinner" started a small engine, then the Cat's diesel engine roared to life with a puff of black smoke. Then two guys climbed up on the combine. I stood there, not sure what to do.

"Climb up on the combine, kid!" said Mr. Vanderveer. I climbed the metal steps as he followed me up to the deck. "You'll be tending header," he said, "and you sit right over here." I walked over to the seat. It was a metal seat, like on a tractor, and I sat on it. There was a big wheel in front of the seat, maybe three feet across, with handles all around.

"You operate the wheel to control the up-and-down moves of the header," he said. The header was a huge box, maybe twenty feet long sticking out from the combine, with rotating paddles herding the wheat stalks into a cutting sickle bar and onto a conveyor belt carrying the stalks inside the machine. "Keep the header about a foot off the ground," he said, "and raise it to miss a big rock or anything else that could cause damage." I nodded and twisted the wheel a couple times to check it out. Then they fired up the combine and the Cat-skinner pulled a handle and the Cat and combine lurched forward. Away we went, belts pounding, chains clanking, header paddles turning, sickle bars flashing and stalks of wheat hitting the conveyor and riding inside and kernels of wheat flying into burlap sacks held up by hooks.

A guy called the "sack-jigger" bounced each sack as it filled up to get it full of wheat before handing it to another guy behind him called the "sack-sewer."

With a long needle and a length of heavy twine, he sewed each sack of wheat with a dozen stitches, leaving two ears of burlap at each side of the full sack. Then he cut the twine with a blade inside the needle and kicked the sack onto a chute running down the side of the combine. When five sacks were lined up, he pulled a handle to drop all five to the ground.

The ride was a little bouncy, but the metal tractor seat fit pretty well and it wasn't too bad. Every so often, I had to yank on the wheel and lift the header to miss a rock. Each time, it gave me a kind of thrill—pride, maybe—that I was doing my part to keep the harvest going. The Cat-skinner kept the Cat and combine going in a straight line—maybe a mile in one direction—before turning a corner and going straight for another mile. We always ran in a clockwise direction around the field and with the uncut wheat always on our right. It took some getting used to, but it wasn't too bad. It was hot out there under the summer sun, sure, and it was noisy with all that cruddy machinery clanking and banging. But most of the time it was okay. The only time it got bad, really bad, was going down a side of the field with a tailwind.

Out the back of the combine spewed a continuous plume of cut-up wheat stalks, mixed with tarweed full of itchy little barbs. A tailwind took this mess and threw it right at your back. It was a hurricane of chaff—so thick you could hardly breathe—mixed with chopped-up tarweed firing millions of tiny little needles into your neck and both sides of your face. Each time we went down a tailwind side, I thought we would never come to the end of the field. Turning a corner and sending the chaff in another direction brought great relief. But the flip side of the coin—what a hopeless feeling—coming down the last leg of the field before turning again into the leg with that awful tailwind!

At noon, we stopped to eat and relax. Mr. Vanderveer's wife drove her car out on the field with a bunch of sandwiches and hot coffee, and we wolfed it down. While we were resting, Mr. Vanderveer fired up the combine and poured oil on the outside chains running over the sprockets. Then it was time to board the combine and roll out once again. We ran all afternoon until, finally, at six o'clock, Mr. Vanderveer called it quits for the day. We had worked about twelve hours and were ready to quit. When we got back to the ranch headquarters, we lined up along a metal trough while somebody pumped water from a well into the trough. I looked into a little mirror hanging there on a nail—my face covered with dirt and chaff—and splashed water all over my face and arms.

Then the cook banged on the metal triangle and we all filed into the cookhouse for dinner. It was a great feast, I had to admit. There were roast beef, mashed potatoes with gravy, corn-on-the-cob, big juicy carrots and ice cream, heaps of ice cream, all you could eat. I found out one thing—a hired hand gets to eat well—always good food and plenty of it.

After a couple of weeks, I settled down into a routine that was sleep, get up, eat, work all day, clean up, eat, sleep, get up, eat, work all day, clean up, etc. etc. Each day of work was followed by another day of work, as we cut through several fields of wheat, leaving deserts of stubbled field and piles of full wheat sacks along the combine tracks.

Most of the time, I sat watching the field ahead, looking for rocks. I sat there hypnotized by those header paddles going round and round and round. I watched the wheat stalks standing innocent as hell, with the combine coming closer and closer, until finally they are gently guided by the nice friendly paddles onto the razor-sharp sickle bar flashing back and forth, cutting off their bodies like guillotines and laying them on the conveyor belt, dead as King Tut now, and carried into the bowels of the combine to be beaten, flailed about, chewed up into tiny bits and spewed out the back, while the precious wheat kernels flew into a burlap sack held by hooks and compacted into full bags of wheat by the sack-jigger.

I could see Mr. Vanderveer was having fun, just riding the combine and watching the wheat pouring in and wheat sacks piling up in the stubble-fields. He wasn't grinning or anything but he sure wasn't pissed-off.

I wondered how much loot he got off each sack of wheat. I wondered how many sacks of wheat he had when the harvest was all over. Harvest was his big payoff; I could see that. I could imagine how nice it was to get those sacks of wheat in a warehouse, sell them and get paid for a whole year's work. I figured working for a whole year and spending lots of cash money on all the stuff that goes into an operation like that, and finally getting paid only after the wheat is harvested and stored in bags in a warehouse and then sold—I figured all that work and gambling on the weather, other things that can screw you up good—well, I just figured all that would qualify Mr.Vanderveer as a great onta-pra-newer right up there with the best of them.

By this time, I had been accepted as a full-fledged member of our crew with genuine friendship all around. Once, when Mr. Vanderveer took off in his pickup to get more burlap sacks, a sack-jigger taught me how to do his job. It wasn't too tough. You just bounced the sack up and down while it was filling up to compact the wheat before handing it off to the sack-sewer and then hooking up wheat. They showed me how to wrap the twine around the right ear and throw a reverse loop, sew a dozen stitches through the sack, wrap the twine around the left ear and throw another reverse loop, jerk the needle back to cut the twine, and kick the finished sack down the chute—all in about ten seconds. It was a great thrill to accomplish this complicated task, thanks to my buddies on the combine crew.

Some evenings after dinner, we sat around an old picnic table under some poplar trees not far from the bunkhouse. I usually just sat and listened to my crew-mates talk about their past lives or their plans for the future. We had been on the harvest over three weeks and everybody got along real good. The sack-jigger and sack-sewer were older guys, with rough and whiskery faces, always rolling up cigarettes, lighting the twisted ends, taking deep drags, coughing and blowing out clouds of smoke.

The Cat-skinner was younger, maybe twenty, always clean-shaven and cheerful, who said he wanted to join the Navy and see the world. One night, they were talking about plans for after the harvest. The sack-jigger and sack-sewer said they were going to Portland and raise some hell.

"Can I ask you something?" I said.

"Sure, kid," said the sack-jigger.

"What's a cathouse?"

A moment of stunned silence broke into roars of laughter. Boy, was I stupid, showing my ignorance like that! The Cat-skinner looked at me like a teacher would. Like Mr. Baxter would, understanding I had a legitimate question needing an answer.

"A cathouse is a whorehouse. It's a place you go to fuck somebody. You pay some money, pick out the girl you want, then screw your brains out."

"You ever screw anybody?" asked the sack-sewer.

I shook my head.

"You oughta try it sometime."

"Is it anything like fooling around?"

"Depends on what you mean by fooling around."

"There was a girl one time who asked me to fool around. Up at East Lake. Only I had to go fishing with my dad."

"You should've grabbed that one," said the Cat-skinner. "You don't get too many chances like that. You should've done something."

"Like what?"

"Make out like you were sick. You should've stuck your fingers down your throat and up-chucked all over the place. Anything to stay on shore."

I nodded sadly in agreement. How many times I wished I had that moment back! If I could do it again, I knew just what I would do. I'd seen myself many times standing on that gravelly shore, waving to Dad and Evelyn in the boat as they skimmed across the water out to the middle of the cruddy lake. I had seen myself many times then waving to the East Lake Girl to meet me at the edge of the woods just up from the beach.

The sack-jigger stood up and stretched. It looked like our group was going to break up and head inside to hit the sack. But first, I had one more question.

"What does it cost?"

"What does what cost?" asked the sack-jigger.

"Cathouse, whorehouse, whatever. And where is it?"

"Bend has four." said the Cat-skinner. "Last I heard, it was three dollars a trick. Shit, that's half a day's pay." Shit, I thought, that's over a full day's pay for me.

The sack-jigger stretched again and crushed out his cigarette. Then everybody stood and walked back to the bunkhouse. I walked down the hallway to my shabby little room and climbed into my stupid sleeping bag.

Lying there, I could hear one of the guys snoring already. Time to get some shut-eye. I was still a miserable little rat out here on this cruddy wheat harvest. But I was real happy to find out—at last—what a cathouse was. And to know, for sure, I had been right about something. When the East Lake Girl said we could fool around, she really meant she wanted me to screw her up in the woods.

Ten

The day after the "whorehouse talk" was a day just like all the other days of the wheat harvest. But on this day, I heard some really great news. The sack-sewer said we were almost near the end of the harvest. Before long, it would be all over. Wow! That was the best news I had ever heard in my entire life! Soon the jail sentence would be over. Soon Mr. Vanderveer would take me back to Madras, back home with my own family, back with Skipper and all the other kids. Soon I would be going back to school again, back with my old friends, near Beverly Nelson again. I was so thrilled; I wasn't even worried about the Mexican. Not much anyway.

The combine kept lurching along through the wheat, leaving its desert of stubble and sacks of wheat, bouncing along toward the final cut in the last field. Then, while I was dreaming away about going back home to Madras—BANG!—came a loud noise from inside the combine. Mr. Vanderveer jumped up and pulled a rope which rang a bell above the Cat-skinner who pulled a lever and stopped us in our tracks. Mr. Vanderveer climbed down, opened a side panel and looked inside.

We had a broken sprocket, he said, and would have to quit for the day while he got it fixed. He was really pissed-off, but nobody else seemed to mind one little bit. In fact, everyone on the crew—including me—seemed kind of happy about it. We all cheerfully climbed into the back of the pickup and rode back to ranch headquarters. With a sour look, Mr. Vanderveer drove away with the precious sprocket beside him.

The Cat-skinner took off in his Dodge sedan and came back about an hour later. He told everyone to jump in his car. We took off with a roar, racing down the back roads of Agency Plains, heading for no particular place. There was a case of cold beer bottles in the back seat. The Cat-skinner said to pass them around.

I took one and looked at it. I had picked up hundreds of these along the highway, back with my ex-partner Mark Collins. The sack-jigger brought out his "church key," popped one open and handed it to the sack-sewer. He took my bottle, popped it open and gave it back. I put my mouth over the open bottle, tipped my head back and swallowed a mouthful. Whew! The taste was awful. I was expecting a sweet taste like Coke—but I managed to drink it down without barfing. The sack-jigger opened another bottle for the Cat-skinner, who grabbed it and took a couple swigs while he careened along the county road.

Then the sack-jigger opened one for himself and took it all down with a couple big swallows. He rolled down his window and tossed his bottle in a long graceful arc. It hit some rocks and busted into a thousand pieces. Then I threw my bottle out and the sack-sewer threw his bottle out and finally the Cat-skinner opened his window and back-handed his bottle over the roof clear out into a field.

Then the sack-sewer took out some cigarette paper and a pouch of tobacco. With the thin paper between his fingers, he dropped a line of tobacco along the paper, licked the paper and rolled it into a cylinder, twisting the ends to hold in the tobacco. He clicked a lighter and the tip flamed and he took a drag of smoke, held it and blew it out. Then he invited me to try it, to roll my own cigarette.

I took the paper, held it between my fingers and shook some tobacco into the tiny little trough. Then I licked one side of the paper and tried to stick it to the other side of the paper. But the whole cruddy mess fell apart and dropped to the floor of the car. The sack-jigger and sack-sewer chuckled in a good-natured way at my clumsy efforts.

The Cat-skinner looked around and smiled. "That's too much work," he said. "I use tailor-mades myself." He pulled out a pack of Lucky Strikes and handed it over to me. I took out a cigarette and gave the pack back to the Cat-skinner. 1 stuck the cigarette in my mouth and the sack-jigger clicked his lighter and lit me up. 1 took a sneaky little drag—hoping 1 looked like the big-shots in the movies—and exhaled before 1 choked on the smoke. 1 had to admit that tailor-mades were a lot easier. It looked like our crew was split right down the middle—one half liked roll-your-own cigarettes and the other half liked tailor-mades.

The sack-jigger opened three more bottles and passed them out, then opened one for himself. Again, he polished off the whole bottle in two swigs. Once again, he tossed the bottle out in a long graceful arc that finished with a shattering crash on a pile of rocks. By then, everyone was laughing, swigging beer, throwing bottles out the window, spilling beer all over themselves and laughing like crazy at every little thing that happened.

This went on for several hours, as we careened around those back-county roads, smoking and drinking beer, throwing empties out the window and laughing ourselves silly. It was great fun. It was the most fun I had all summer, if you want to know the truth. I had to wonder, though, what Mom would've thought if she had seen me in action during this particular "character-building" episode.

By the end of the week, we had finished the wheat harvest. Back at the bunkhouse, I rolled up my sleeping bag and packed all the other stuff into my gym bag. Then I washed up and walked over to the cookhouse for one more supper. It was the most satisfying meal of the whole month. After the cherry pie, I went round, shook hands and said goodbye to my crew-mates. I told the Cat-skinner I hoped he would get to join the Navy and see the world. I told the sack-jigger and the sack-sewer I hoped they had lots of fun raising hell in Portland.

Then I picked up my sleeping bag and gym bag and climbed into Mr. Vanderveer's pickup for the ride back to Madras. When we pulled up in front of my house, it looked like a palace. I grabbed my stuff, shook hands with Mr. Vanderveer and said good-bye. He drove away as I walked up the driveway. I was home again—the happiest kid in the whole world!

It was great to be living like an ordinary kid again, having meals at regular times, going to sleep in my own bed again, and not having to work twelve hours a day. When Mom got my paycheck, she helped me set up a bank account. I spent some on school clothes and kept most of it in the bank, making sure to have enough cash on hand to take in a movie whenever I wanted. Mostly, I was happy just being a regular school kid again. Now, I was finally a full-fledged eighth grader. I was sitting on top of the world and most of the time I never even worried about that damned Mexican.

~ * ~

One of the first movies I saw after getting back home, was *The Grapes of Wrath* starring Henry Fonda. It was based on a book by John Steinbeck and it was really depressing. The movie was about a family in Oklahoma who lose everything in the Dust Bowl. Their house goes back to the bank which has it knocked over by a bulldozer. They load up the whole family in a rattletrap old truck and head west for California. On the way, they run into people who treat them badly and sometimes with pity as they go chugging through New Mexico and Arizona. In California, they get shafted by big farm corporations and beat up by the cops. In the last scene, Ma Joad says, "They can't wipe us out. We'll go on forever, Pa, 'cause we're the people."

During the movie, I kept thinking about my Okie friend, Jake Hartley, and his family in that little tarpaper shack back in Redmond. The movie made me realize what they went through. But I had a good feeling they would eventually come through in great shape.

After Labor Day, school started up again. Skipper and I had no problem getting there—we just walked down "B" Street to the Madras Grade School. It was a straight shot, about eight blocks, and it only took about twenty minutes.

I tried to forget about the Mexican, but it was no use. Why did he follow me from town to town? What did he want from me? What did those cards mean? Four cards, all in spades. What did they mean?

It was great to see my old buddies again, especially Beverly Nelson. I missed Todd McKinney, though. He wasn't there because he had moved on to high school. There were some new kids who came in by car from Warm Springs. They were real friendly and good-looking and fit right in. They were said to be Sioux tribal members, and for some reason living on the Warm Springs Reservation.

Mr. Baxter was back on stage each morning with his lectures on world affairs. He kept us up-to-speed on Germany's invasion of Russia and their push eastward across the map. He showed us how the front lines ran from Leningrad up north to the Crimean Peninsula in the south. By October, heavy rains had bogged the German Army down in the mud. By December, snow and blizzards and sub-zero temperatures had frozen all their equipment and stopped them in their tracks.

We had a visit one day from Mr. Nygaard, the high school band director. He wore horn-rimmed glasses and had long black hair that covered his ears and collar and came down to a crazy duck-tail in the back. It was a good thing he was a music man, or the local rednecks would've given him a hard time. But his long hair showed everybody that he knew all about music and was a first-class musician. Mr. Nygaard said they needed more band players and he was looking for kids to learn to play the different instruments.

I thought maybe I could learn to play something. My old enemy Collins went for the drums, which suited him about right. As for me, I had seen a Benny Goodman movie, so I chose the clarinet. Mr. Nygaard said he could arrange lessons for any kids wanting to learn. Mom said clarinet lessons were fine if I practiced before Dad came home in the evening, that was okay. So she bought me a second-hand metal job and I started taking lessons from Mr. Nygaard. Of course, he was also teaching many other kids with lots of different instruments. With all those kids paying for lessons, he must have tripled his band director income. What an onta-pra-newer!

Before I hardly knew which end of the horn to blow on, Mr. Nygaard stuck me and the other beginners in the high school band. Then he arranged a concert at the high school gym. Maybe Mr. Nygaard wanted to prove to the parents how their kids were making real progress in show business.

Being loaded with money, I took in a bunch of movies on weekends. Going to a movie helped me take my mind off that Mexican. At least for a while. *How Green Was My Valley* was about a coal-mining family in Wales, with Roddy McDowell as the kid and Donald Crisp as the old coal-mining father. Another good movie was *Abe Lincoln of Illinois* starring Raymond Massey as young Lincoln. Some movies weren't so serious. *Sun Valley Serenade* had John Payne chasing Sonja Henie and introduced the song "Chattanooga Choo-Choo." In *The Maltese Falcon,* Humphrey Bogart is a detective who tangles with those evil-doers Sydney Greenstreet and Peter Lorre. *Dr. Jekyll and Mr. Hyde* had Spencer Tracy as a doctor whose experiments turn him into the savage Mr. Hyde who terrorizes the citizens of Edinburgh.

I really liked the easy-going comedies. One of these was *Road to Singapore* with Bob Hope and Bing Crosby as two sailors whose friendship hits the rocks when they both fall for Dorothy Lamour. A comedy seeming to poke fun at some big problems was *The Great Dictator* starring Charlie Chaplin. This one involved a country (maybe Germany?) under a comic leader who looks like Adolph Hitler. In one scene, Chaplin bounces a stupid global balloon around his office while dreaming of world conquest. In another, he tears all the medals off a Hermann Goering look-alike.

Among Madras movie fans, the gold medal belonged to a family of three—an old mother and two middle-age sons—living in a rickety shack just outside the Highway Department fence on the banks of dried-out Willow Creek. They were said to be nut cases and genetic fruitcakes. But they did manage to scrape out a living without doing much work. Somehow, they had acquired a complete Salvation Army uniform. Every so often, one of the brothers would dress up in the uniform and make the rounds downtown, rattling his tambourine in the tavern and in the stores, getting enough donations to live on until the next mission along the Salvation Army trail.

Just about every night, this family came to the Chief Theater and plunked themselves down on the front row. Their scummy body odor kept all others at bay, at least five rows back—that was okay because nobody wanted to sit that close to the screen anyway. Throughout the entire movie, they loudly discussed the characters or the setting or perhaps a twist of the plot—more or less in the manner of newspaper movie critics—but delivered live and with the zeal of true devotees. Their commentary and insights usually provided more pleasure than the show itself, and people often attended movies just to soak up their brilliant insights. Perhaps the owner knew this and maybe gave them free admission as an "Added Attraction."

The Willow Creek family let it all hang out during a movie called *Sergeant York* starring Gary Cooper on some mission and captures hundreds or Germans. After the war, he gets medals from a bunch of different countries. Arriving back in America, he rides in a New York ticker-tape parade and stays at Cooper. They seemed to feel a special kinship with young Alvin York, a hard-drinking hillbilly trying to scratch out a living in the Tennessee badlands. Urged on by preacher Walter Brennan, Cooper turns to religion and his fortunes improve. Hunting wild turkeys, he develops a special turkey call that brings out the gobblers. When America enters the First World War, Cooper as York wants to stay out because "killin' is against the Bible." But he gets talked into joining up anyway. At boot camp, his superiors are amazed at his rifle-shooting abilities. Over in France, his sharp-shooting skills pay off big time. During a battle, he uses his turkey call to bring up enemy heads from the trenches—to the roaring delight of the front-row critics—and he goes on to the Waldorf-Astoria and gets lots of offers for advertising endorsements.

I thought it was kinda strange having this war movie come out just when it looked like we were going to have another big war dropped in our lap. But it was only a coincidence, I guess, that they made the movie when they did. It made war look glamorous, sure, and showed that killing all those Germans was okay, even for a religious guy. It showed that any ordinary Joe could be a national hero with a ticker-tape parade in New York and stay at the Waldorf-Astoria and get those great money-making advertising deals.

~ * ~

Back at school, Mr. Baxter decided to organize a basketball team to compete with other grade-school teams around central Oregon. He assigned me the position of guard in the lineup. When a package arrived at home, it was a big thrill to open it and find my own fancy satin uniform with my very own number on the back of the shirt.

After we practiced for a couple weeks, the season started. From then on, every Friday after lunch, Mr. Baxter drove us to a school in some distant town—Warm Springs or Culver or Sisters—to play their team. It was lots of fun, especially since we got to skip class. But I was especially excited when we drove clear down to LaPine to play a game. I had a hunch that the East Lake Girl lived in LaPine, so I spent much of the game checking out the crowd to see if I could spot her. But I never saw her. For some stupid reason, I kept thinking she must be living in LaPine.

~ * ~

One Saturday morning, Dad said it was time for me to learn how to drive. Awesome! I would be able to drive a car like Todd McKinney! We drove east about ten miles out in the desert on a gravel road. Dad parked and we traded places. I was behind the wheel, motor running, ready to drive our stick-shift Plymouth.

"Okay," said Dad, "the right pedal is the brake—you push that to stop. The left pedal is the clutch. Got that?" I nodded. "Okay, now let out the clutch." I recognized this as the engineering talk which tripped up Mom when she tried to learn.

"You mean shove in the clutch pedal?"

"Yeah, shove in the clutch pedal."

I shoved in the clutch pedal. "Now imagine the letter H," he said.

"The little bar in the middle is Neutral. That's where it is right now. The upper left point is Reverse. The lower left point is First. The upper right point is Second. The lower right point is Third. To shift from one point to another, always shove in the clutch pedal first."

He let that sink in.

"Now, to go forward, you start at First, release the clutch pedal and run a short way, shove in the clutch pedal and shift to Second, then release the clutch pedal and run a little faster, shove in the clutch pedal and shift to Third and you're rolling along at top speed. Got that?" I nodded.

"Ready to try it?" I nodded again.

"Okay, now, shift into First." I shoved in the clutch pedal and pulled the gearshift down to First. I gave it some gas and let up on the clutch pedal, and—it worked!—the car jerked into motion and started rolling down the road! I shoved in the clutch pedal, shifted into Second, and released the pedal—faster yet! I shoved in the clutch pedal again, gave it more gas, shifted to Third, released the pedal and we were barreling down the road!

I yanked the steering wheel back and forth, just to try it, and almost ran off the road. "Careful," said Dad, "keep it straight and narrow." After a mile or so, he said "Okay. Get ready to stop. Push down slowly on both the clutch and the brake." I did like he said and we gradually came to a stop. After that, we practiced all afternoon, going through the gears, coming to a stop and starting up again. By evening, I had it down cold. I knew I could slide in behind the driver's seat any time Dad said it was okay and drive for miles on those back roads.

~ * ~

Later that fall, I discovered why Dad was so anxious to have me learn to drive. He had permission from some ranchers to hunt pheasants on their land. Soon as hunting season opened, he took me with him. We drove out to some bottomland ranch country and stopped along the road. He got out and put on his hunting vest full of shells, grabbed his shotgun, and climbed over a fence. He said to meet him two or three miles down the road. Then he loaded his gun and started walking through the field. I drove down the road a couple miles and parked at a wide spot where he would come out.

While I was waiting for Dad to walk the two or three miles, I had plenty of time to think about stuff. At first, I just laid down outside on a grassy spot to soak up some sun. I soon got tired of that and climbed back in the car. I looked around at the whole scene. The countryside was a broad ribbon of green pasture and alfalfa fields alongside a creek that ran through a shallow canyon out in the middle of the desert rangeland. The sky was real blue, blue as Crater Lake, like somebody had painted it with deep blue dye from horizon to horizon. It was that blue, with no clouds to spoil it. And quiet. Quiet as hell. Peaceful and quiet. Not a sound. Out across the pastureland, I could see some cattle grazing. Herefords, I think, but anyway who gives a damn what they were. Just standing out there, heads right down in the grass, not moving one little bit. You couldn't even tell if they were real or just some stuffed animals some smart-ass stuck out there. In the distance, I could see a house and a barn, but no sign of anybody around. Everything real peaceful and quiet. No people, no cattle moving, no sound of any kind—

BANG! BANG! BANG! Three shots. Holy crap, that must've been Dad shooting up the place. It sounded like a war starting up, those shots. He must've shot a couple pheasants. He'll be showing up with a couple of dead pheasants in his hunting vest. To tell the truth, I really hated the idea of shooting those birds.

They look so damn pretty, pheasants do, with all those colored feathers and that long colored tail hanging out behind. When you flush 'em out, they take off with a wild eruption of feathers flapping and squawking that scares the heck out of you. Exciting as hell. The first time I heard that, I was Dad's bird dog wading along a ditch full of deep grass while he walked on the bank above. I flushed three big roosters at one time and Dad got so excited it's a wonder he didn't shoot me or himself. Trouble is, after you kill a pheasant, you gotta take it home. You have to pull out all those beautiful feathers and cut off its beautiful head and what you have left is a shriveled-up carcass that doesn't even taste as good as chicken.

All that heavy thinking about pheasants getting killed made me think about the war going on in Europe. It looked like they were killing people over there for no good reason. Just like Dad getting his jollies killing all those beautiful pheasants. Looked like the Germans were to blame. I couldn't understand why Germans, people like my old neighbor Mr. Fenstermacher, would be invading Russia and killing all kinds of people. It just didn't make any sense that a nice old guy like him would go on a rampage across Europe blowing up buildings and killing people. Maybe he had seen this war coming and that's why he came to America.

Maybe he was glad to get out of there, having nothing to do with the war. But maybe America couldn't keep out of it. Dad always said we'd get sucked into it sooner or later, one way or another. It was kinda funny. He always said he didn't like war and thought it was the most stupid thing in the world. He always said the idea of killing people made him sick. Killing pheasants, that's okay, but not killing people. I guess he figured that pheasants were made to be shot and killed, but not people.

"Well, I got a couple," Dad said. I jumped, startled by his voice. I was thinking so hard about him and the pheasants, I didn't even notice him coming up to the fence by the road, clearing his gun and. climbing over the fence. Sure enough, he had a couple of beautiful roosters in his hunting vest. It was kinda funny. He seemed real happy, almost as happy as the time we went to that burlesque show in Portland. What did those two deals have in common to make him so happy? Excitement, I guess. Maybe he got bored planning those highways and doing all that math and drawing lines on all those stupid charts.

On the way back, we didn't talk much. Dad was driving along, lost in happy memories of his hunting trip. For some reason, I got to thinking about that damned Mexican. I wondered if he watched me every day. I wondered if he had followed us out there to the bottomlands. I wondered if he had set up a lookout on the ridge, watching us from behind some sagebrush and rocks.

Every so often, he got into my head like that. But lately I had calmed down a little bit about it. I wasn't as freaked out as I was at first. I wasn't as scared of him as I was before. He could've grabbed me or even stabbed me by now if he'd wanted to. It wasn't much, but this idea gave me a little comfort, so I could hang in there and maybe not be so worried about it.

~ * ~

Sometimes on weekends, Skipper and I went on expeditions with Dad to roam around the outback countryside looking for fossils. Usually this meant finding a place along a county road where they cut through a sandstone formation. When he saw something that looked promising, he stopped the car and we got out. With his pickaxe, Dad chipped away at the sandstone while we watched. Sometimes he uncovered the end of a fossil. Then we spent all day digging all around it to pick up a chunk of bone and sandstone to take home for more careful cleaning.

One Sunday in December, Skipper and I rode with Dad several miles out in the desert to look for fossils again. We came to a sandstone cut and stopped. Dad got out and started looking over the formation as usual, chipping away with his pickaxe. He let out a whistle—he had discovered a large bone. We helped him chip the sandstone away from the bone. But this one was much bigger than usual. As we chipped away, we could see smaller bones branching out from it.

As usual, we had to remove all of it, bone and sandstone, to take home and clean up. This time he planned to ship the fossil over to the University of Oregon. So we chipped away, trying to dig around it enough to get the whole thing out of the ground and into our car.

Suddenly Dad stood and checked his watch.

"I promised to get back before noon," he said. "I promised to drive Mom to some church meeting."

So we left the fossil where it was. We picked up all the tools, got back in the car and drove home. Skipper and 1 ran inside, laughing and clowning around.

Mom said to quiet down. Her favorite radio show, the *Mormon Tabernacle Choir*, had been interrupted for some kind of announcement.

We all sat in the living room and looked at the Philco floor radio. We sat and stared at the walnut curlicues and soft-woven mesh over the speakers. What followed were words we would never forget.

"We interrupt this program to bring you a special news bulletin. The Japanese have attacked Pearl Harbor, in Hawaii. Japanese airplanes have attacked the U. S. Naval Fleet at Pearl Harbor. We repeat this announcement. The Japanese have attacked Pearl Harbor..."

We sat there, stunned.

"How could those Japs have the guts to attack us like that?" said Dad.

"Pearl Harbor?" I said. "I never heard of it."

All day long, we sat and stared at the radio. We learned more about the attack, about the casualties and the ships sunk or damaged. There were reports of the entire West Coast going on full alert against a possible invasion. There were stories about men lining up to enlist in the Army, Navy and Marines. This news was repeated over and over. We just sat, listened and tried to understand what had happened and wondered what would happen next.

The next day, school was cancelled so we could stay home and listen to President Roosevelt address a joint session of Congress. We listened in awe as he spoke the words which summed up the feelings of everyone:

"Yesterday, December 7, 1941—a date which will live in infamy—the United States of America was suddenly and deliberately attacked by naval and air forces of the Empire of Japan."

We never went back to the big fossil. That fossil we found had been waiting for ten million years to get discovered and dug out. It's probably still there, still waiting, probably for another ten million years.

Eleven

Pearl Harbor changed everything. Suddenly we were at war with Japan and Germany and even Italy. At first, everybody thought it would be a great adventure that brought the good times back. The wise old bastards who knew everything said it would be all wrapped up by Christmas of next year. Radio commentators and newspaper experts said the Japs were stupid and nearsighted. Cartoons pictured them as bow-legged little cretins with buck-tooth grins and Coke-bottle glasses.

Only the propaganda didn't square with the news. In no time, the Japs swept over southeast Asia. Wake Island gave up and Thailand surrendered, plus Hong Kong and Guam. Japanese troops advanced into Malaysia and Burma. Singapore surrendered in February and the Dutch East Indies fell in March. The U.S. Army, fighting Japan's invasion of the Philippines, retreated to the Bataan Peninsula and Corregidor Island. Places we never heard of became etched in our minds forever.

Back in this country, draft boards registered and screened all eligible men and mailed out notices to report for active duty. People in Madras, like everywhere, put up with all kinds of lousy shortages. Dad got an "A" sticker for the car and coupons to buy four gallons of gas a week. Other coupon books rationed the buying of cheese, sugar, coffee, flour, fish, and canned goods. They even rationed beef, holding everyone to twenty-eight ounces a week.

This rule seemed really stupid—when you could drive out and see huge herds of cattle grazing—but it was wartime and nobody complained too much about it. They started a big campaign to have folks grow "victory gardens." Drives were held to collect all kinds of stuff. First it was rubber. They wanted anything made of rubber—old tires and rubber boots—then they wanted aluminum pans and old newspapers and scrap iron. Little old Madras collected lots of this stuff. Especially scrap iron. Before long, piles of scrap iron were building up in the vacant lot behind the Chief Theater.

By that time, I had gotten to know Chuck Foster of Redmond. He was tall and lanky, like Dad, and liked to laugh a lot. My sister Evelyn was dating him and sometimes he came over for dinner. Next thing I knew, they got engaged and were set to get married on Valentine's Day. The wedding was low-key, family members only, held in the living room of our house in Madras. Mom had some photographer take some stupid pictures, including a family portrait.

We were all dressed up, but I had to turn my head to hide a black eye picked up the day before. Another fight with Collins. Don't ask me what caused it. He just came up after school and hit me with a sucker punch without warning. I gave him some good shots right back. Never had a clue what was eating him. He was a weird kid that way.

Dad was especially helpful that morning. He told Evelyn they were crazy to get married during wartime. That set off a big brawl, words flying like shrapnel, so everyone was really pissed-off and miserable when the photographer showed up. Everyone except Skipper, who secretly enjoyed the fracas and fondly soaked up every cutting remark and sarcastic comeback. Right after the wedding, Evelyn and Chuck left for Timberline Lodge on Mount Hood. It was good that they didn't know anyone in Madras or Jefferson County. Especially a group of ranchers, whose main entertainment was acting out another stupid pioneer custom long since forgotten everywhere else. It was called "shivaree," a supposedly good-natured harassment of the bride and groom striving to consummate their marital vows.

Had they known the newlyweds, these masterminds would've followed them all the way up to the lodge, banging on their door and shooting off fireworks in the snow outside their window. In Madras, a shivaree was considered a sacred art form and high social event. At church dinners and school picnics, I'd heard these worthies describe their escapades with the zeal of deer hunters reciting every last little detail of a successful hunt.

Not long after the wedding, Chuck received his "Greetings" letter from the draft board and soon after was called into active duty. Evelyn bought a car and followed him everywhere across the country, setting up housekeeping in a series of little Army towns. Eventually, he was shipped out to the Pacific. He was stationed on some island, helping build landing strips for Air Corps B-29s to bomb the Japanese home islands.

In spite of—or because of—the onset of war, 1942 was maybe the wackiest year in Oregon history. Right after Pearl Harbor, Governor Sprague declared Oregon a "combat zone." The Portland *Oregonian* said, "our citizens are duty-bound to prepare ourselves as though the war may be at our beaches." Plans called for east-west highways to be reserved for civilian evacuation, and north-south highways set for military traffic in case of a Japanese invasion.

Anti-Japanese hysteria caused federal authorities to "exclude" all citizens of Japanese ancestry living in west coast states. Loyal Americans, they lost their freedom, along with their homes and farms. The eastern line of exclusion was Highway 97 running north-south through the middle of Oregon and right through the center of Madras. The sheriff was ordered to round up all Japanese-Americans living west of the highway. Those on the east side of the highway were okay. Those on the west side were deemed potential spies and saboteurs and sent to concentration camps.

One such family lived on the Warm Springs Indian Reservation. There was a father of Japanese ancestry, an Indian mother, and eight children, of whom the oldest was a boy, serving in the U.S. Army. It presented a brand-new problem in ethnic cleansing and a brand-new headache for federal officers. After much deliberation, they handed down a ruling—since the Warm Springs Indian Reservation was west of Highway 97—this family, too, must be taken from their home and sent to a concentration camp.

The talk in town seemed to favor shipping Japanese-Americans to the camps. I heard this once: "If the Japs didn't want to get shipped out, they shouldn't have bombed Pearl Harbor." Okay, that made sense. Only what about the Warm Springs family? Did the Indians bomb Pearl Harbor? In my opinion, I thought they should just leave the Warm Springs family alone. With seven kids underfoot, how could they have any time to spy on anybody or sabotage anything?

From Astoria in the north to Brookings in the south, rumors spread along the coast about imminent attacks on Oregon beaches. Vigilante groups were formed by loggers, fishermen and shopkeepers to help fight off the coming invasion. They called themselves "guerrillas" and took their duties very seriously. They formed units such as the Siuslaw Rifles of Florence, the Newport Guerrillas, and a group known as Company A, Lincoln County Guerrillas. They brought in deer rifles and shotguns to march in formation, to hold close-order drills, and for target practice. They made plans to blow up tunnels and bridges along Highway 101. They laid down barbed wire on the beaches above the high-tide line and patrolled along the wire with their rifles and shotguns. A tourist wouldn't be too smart to come splashing in through the waves, yelling and waving his arms. That would be really stupid. Any tourist would be well-advised to keep a low profile, maybe just visiting some lighthouses or having clam chowder at some little dive someplace.

Editorial writers loved the volunteers and the spirit they brought to the war effort. One paper said "tough high-climbers and donkey-punchers from logging camps, sawmill workers, and farmers skilled on the duck marsh and deer trails flocked in to form guerrilla companies." The *Oregonian* said, "These ranchers, woodsmen, and loggers are riflemen to the last man-Jack of them, for whom a deer glimpsed on the run is meat in. the pot."

Eventually, the Oregon vigilantes caught national attention. *Life* magazine published a full-page shot of two Tillamook guerrilla snipers hiding behind a stump protecting a logging road near Sandlake. Chicago *Daily News:* "If we were a Jap, we wouldn't pick Tillamook for a landing. We wouldn't want to find lumberjacks with rifles in their hands amidst Douglas firs" Other papers carried the photo and movie-goers everywhere saw newsreel accounts of the volunteers. Even the British press picked up on it. The London *Sunday Dispatch* ran the Tillamook photo with a caption: "One thousand American backwoodsmen meet in Oregon to organize a new type hunt—not wild game, but of any Japanese who lands on the west coast of America."

Many Oregon people served as watchers in the Aircraft Warning Service. They studied silhouettes of Japanese bombers and learned how to tell a Mitsubishi "Betty" from a Mitsubishi "Sally." All drivers had to keep their headlights on low and hold their speed down to 40 mph on the main highways.

In cities and towns throughout the Willamette Valley, there was a big drive to screw up the Japanese bombers by dousing all lights at night. These "blackout" efforts involved hastily enacted laws against neon signs, street lights and every shred of illumination from every home. Wardens in doughboy helmets patrolled the streets, looking for any slackers whose house lights would give Japanese bombardiers an easy target. Luckily, none of this blackout craze reached Madras where street lights and neon signs and house lights blazed merrily away. In this case, common sense finally came through. Someone among the Powers-That-Be decided that little old Madras just wasn't worth bombing.

~ * ~

Back in school, my classmates and I were busy working our way through the eighth grade. We studied all the usual grade school stuff, plus soaking up the daily lectures by Mr. Baxter. I really had to admire this guy who could stand up there for sixty minutes each day giving his State of the Union address, looking to the left and looking to the right, talking on and on about life and people he had known. I tried to keep up my "romance" with Beverly Nelson by writing her notes and talking with her at recess. That was about as much traction as I could get, since she went home each night to her ranch. I couldn't take her to a movie, for God's sake, or even buy her a Coke at the drug store. Even though I could drive, I was years away from getting a driver's license. So I couldn't even borrow the Plymouth and drive out on a weekend to see her.

Meanwhile, I kept up my clarinet lessons and kept on playing that stupid metal horn back in the clarinet loser section of the high school band. Early in the year, we gave our first concert of the season. I sat up on the stage with the others, trying to follow the music and hoping I wouldn't squawk out some bad notes at the wrong time.

By then, the basketball season was in full swing. I played the same guard position as the year before and had the same team-mates. Every Friday afternoon, we skipped class and rode with Coach Baxter for a game over at Warm Springs or Culver or Sisters, sometimes even going clear down to LaPine. For some reason, I felt sure the East Lake Girl lived somewhere around LaPine. So naturally I spent the whole game staring into the crowd trying to spot her. But no such luck.

Suddenly, the war news got better. In April of 1942, Colonel Doolittle led a bombing attack on Tokyo, flying B-25 bombers off an aircraft carrier. In May, a Japanese invasion group, heading for Australia was met by an American naval force in the Battle of the Coral Sea. Then came the first big victory in the Pacific. In June, the U.S. Navy scored a decisive win at the Battle of Midway. When it was over, Navy fliers had sunk four Japanese carriers—the same carriers which had launched the attack on Pearl Harbor six months earlier.

That spring, our school staged an operetta called *The Magic Piper* with my classmates and me wearing *papier-mâché* rat heads and burlap costumes with long tails. It was based on the Pied Piper story, the guy who plays his flute and leads all the rats out of town. When he gets double-crossed by the city fathers, he plays his flute again and leads all the kids out of town.

Almost every eighth-grader had a role to play, including Beverly Nelson. In the rat outfit, I scooted over next to her during rehearsals. I even put my arm around her when the teacher wasn't looking. Just a touch of romance. A rat's share. Not much, but better than nothing.

I tried to figure out the takeaway lessons from this *Magic Flute* story. I finally decided it was "Never Trust City Hall. If You Do Trust City Hall, You Will Get Shafted. If You Do Get Shafted, Get Even."

One day, it was announced that Portland Flying Service would move from Portland to the county airport, a landing strip in the wheat fields up on Agency Plains. The news caused great excitement, with merchants rubbing their hands over the new dollars coming in and women's clubs busy making plans to welcome the cadets and keep them happy when off-duty. Road engineers began working on plans to widen and extend the runway to handle trainer planes. City fathers got into the act, converting the water district office into a recreation center for the cadets. Mr. Baxter gave a speech at the dedication ceremony, turning his head to the left and to the right. His address to the assembled multitude was about the importance of recreation for our boys in the service.

~ * ~

In other ways, life in wartime Madras continued on the same track it had followed for generations. One day, McKinney came down from high school and invited me along to watch the end of a criminal trial at the Jefferson County courthouse. I got permission to skip class and we walked the four blocks from the school to the courthouse.

Inside the cool interior, McKinney led the way up the staircase and along a corridor. He pushed open a door and I followed him into the courtroom. The court was in session and you could tell it had very serious matters to consider. Sitting up front on a raised platform behind a big desk was the judge in his black robe. Guys all dressed up in suits were sitting at two tables on the lower level, and a jury of other men in suits sat on two levels along one side of the room.

One of the jury members stood up, holding a paper. The defendant, sitting at a lower table, got to his feet. He was smaller than the others and he was wearing an ill-fitting suit. The little man seemed all shriveled-up and out-of-place, like he didn't belong in the company of these proud men in the jury and at the tables.

"What is your verdict?" asked the judge.

"Guilty, Your Honor," said the man with the paper.

The little man slumped even more as the judge sentenced him to ten years in the state penitentiary. As the bailiffs marched him by, I saw his eyes welled up with tears.

McKinney had a strange triumphant look on his face. He said the man had been a hired hand at his ranch for many years. Then he and McKinney got into an argument over something and the man got fired. One night the man sneaked back to the ranch. In the barn, he found McKinney's saddle and chopped it up with an axe. They knew right away who had done it. All the sheriff had to do was find the guy.

Now I understood all the passion behind this trial. In Madras, the code of the Old West still prevailed. Men may be fighting and dying in battles overseas, but folks back home needed to maintain the sacred rule of law. Chopping up a man's saddle with an axe? Clearly a most heinous crime committed by a desperado who deserved to spend many years behind bars. A capital crime, most certainly, akin to murder or rustling, and one that needed to be dealt with in the finest tradition of frontier justice.

One day at school, Mr. Baxter talked about the subtle difference between people who are crazy and those who are feeble-minded. He said crazy people—those he called "manic-depressive" or "schizophrenic"—were often people of high intelligence who had slipped over the edge. He contrasted those "psychotics" with the mentally retarded folks who had labels like "idiot," "moron" or "imbecile," according to their levels of subnormal intelligence. He said the latter group had faulty genes passed down from generation to generation.

As he talked about this, I thought about the mother and two sons living in the shack over by Willow Creek. Everybody said they were crazy, but maybe they were just retarded. Then I thought about how the brothers got that phony Salvation Army outfit and wore it into town rattling their tambourine and collecting enough money to live on. It seemed like a pretty clever stunt to me. I wondered just how crazy or retarded they really were.

Whatever box they belonged in, they knew how to entertain folks attending movies at the Chief Theater. They were there every night down on the front row, passing judgment on the story, the characters or the acting, a distinguished level of film criticism seldom found elsewhere. It was especially comforting to witness the consistency of their pronouncements. Without much fanfare, a movie called *Algiers* came to town. It starred Charles Boyer as a big-time criminal hiding out in the Casbah section of Algiers, along with his gang of thugs and crooks. One day, Hedy Lamarr shows up as a tourist off a cruise ship in the harbor. She runs into Boyer while taking a tour through the maze of passageways and tunnels of this mysterious old quarter. Somehow, she gets separated from the other tourists and Boyer takes over from there.

The Willow Creek family was watching from the front row, offering their usual commentary on the setting, story line and acting. Then Boyer and Lamarr get into a steamy love scene. The Willow Creek family was silent for several moments. But the older brother became agitated, wriggling around in the seat. "Mush!" he yelled suddenly, jumping to his feet and storming up the aisle. "Mush!" he yelled again, halfway up the aisle, and "Mush!" again as he angrily brushed aside the entry curtains and disappeared through the lobby and outdoors into the night. Those who kept track of such things were not surprised to find all of them back again the next night for the same show. Sure enough, at the same scene, the older brother stormed out again, yelling "Mush!" once or twice before plunging out through the entry curtains. In fact, he stormed out in the same fashion at the same scene during the entire week the movie was playing in Madras. With this family, you could always count on a steadfast devotion to whatever principles were guiding their judgments.

The movies which came out that year seemed to provide just the right touch of deliverance from the war news. Such as *Woman of the Year* with Spencer Tracy and Katharine Hepburn. Gary Cooper played Lou Gehrig in *Pride of the Yankees.* Two favorites were *Yankee Doodle*

Dandy, starring James Cagney, and *Holiday Inn* with Bing Crosby, who introduced the song "White Christmas." When these films came to the Chief Theater, they were honestly scrutinized, with verdicts faithfully rendered by the family of three from the little shack on the banks of dried-out Willow Creek.

One movie came along so powerful it shut them up for all but the final scene. It was *Mrs. Miniver* with Greer Garson and Walter Pidgeon, about an English family on the outbreak of the war. They live in a storybook house next to a river, with a cabin cruiser docked nearby, in an idyllic little village near London. It's the summer of 1939 and everything is great. Everyone is friendly and cheerful, in the pubs and in church, as they plan for the annual flower show. After shopping in London, Garson runs into the local duchess and vicar, or preacher, on the train ride back home. The Minivers' oldest son, Vin, is home from college and dating the duchess' granddaughter. So far, so good.

Then war is declared on Germany. Soon after that come the air raids. Vin shows up in an RAF outfit and says he's been training as a fighter pilot. One night, Walter Pidgeon is called out on some secret mission. He is told to run his boat down the river, joining thousands of other boats. They cross the English Channel in a huge armada to rescue thousands of British Army troops from Dunkirk.

While her husband is gone, Garson discovers a wounded German pilot who has parachuted into her garden. With his gun, he orders her into the house. Then he passes out, so she grabs his gun and calls the cops, who take him away. When Pidgeon gets back, he smirks around in his new-found glory until he finds out about the German pilot. Later, the family hides out in their backyard shelter while bombs destroy their house. Vin comes home on leave with his new bride, the duchess' granddaughter. After another London air raid, Vin is ordered back on duty. Garson and the new bride take him to the airfield. Driving home, they get strafed by a German plane and the bride is killed.

This tear-jerker sets up the final scene. At the Sunday church service, the vicar gives a rousing speech: "They say this is the people's war. Very well, we will fight it then!" and they sing "Onward Christian Soldiers" as the camera looks skyward through the bombed-out roof of the cathedral to see a squadron of Spitfires heading off to meet the German Luftwaffe bombers and fighter planes. When the lights came back on, the crowd jumped to its feet and burst into applause. I had never seen that happen at a movie. Even the Willow Creek family was standing and applauding. It was probably just a coincidence, but that movie came out at just the right time to get everybody fired up about the war effort. No doubt everyone who saw that movie wanted to whip the Germans real bad. Even more so than the Japs. As for me, all I could do was cuss myself for being too damned young to enlist in the Army, Navy or Marines right then and there.

~ * ~

Eventually the school year came to a screeching halt. In June, Madras Grade School staged a very important event—graduation of the Class of 1942. After a rousing speech by Mr. Baxter—Iooking to his left and looking to his right—we stood up, one by one, and marched to the front and up on the stage to receive our hard-earned grade school diplomas.

In honor of this majestic occasion, Mom organized a party. Right after the ceremony, the parents drove their kids to our place. I was thrilled to see Beverly Nelson walk into my house. She was wearing a dark-blue velvet dress, making her look even better than usual.

With the grownups sitting in the living room munching cookies and drinking coffee, I took the kids upstairs to play some party games. We went into my bedroom and sat around on the floor. We played "Charades" for a while. It was fun, but I wanted more excitement. I set up a "Spin The Bottle" game in which a girl gets kissed if the bottle points at her. The first spin of the bottle ended up—surprise!—pointing at Beverly. I gave her a good long kiss. She didn't seem to mind, so I turned out the lights and took her hand and we moved over to a corner. In the dark, I knew other kids had started necking. I gave Beverly a passionate kiss and then another. I ran my hands over the outside of her dress and up and down her legs and over her front, even the soft spots, and she didn't back off one bit! Awesome! I kept kissing her and running my hands up her back and all over the front of her dress and down her legs and she didn't stop me! Oh, if I only had a stupid driver's license and could borrow the family car and—

"Hamilton!" Mom yelled up the stairs. "The party is over!"

Oh, crap! I got up and turned on the lights and caught other guys kissing girls who weren't fighting back either. Soon as the lights came on, the girls jumped up and straightened their dresses and the boys wiped lipstick off their mouths. We all walked downstairs to the entry hall. I waved goodbye to everybody as they were leaving. Beverly was standing there, looking at me in a thoughtful way. I walked her out to her parents' car. She got in and waved goodbye as they drove away. It had been lots of fun. But then I felt a deep pain in my crotch, a pain I never had before. I puked right into the grass. What was going on? My crotch still hurt like hell. It hurt so bad I could hardly walk. I limped back inside and started climbing up the steps in great pain. Skipper saw me and laughed, thinking I was clowning around. Clowning around like hell. In fact, I could hardly make it up there, one painful step at a time. Where did this come from? From all that heavy necking? I guess that was my body saying, "Don't start something unless you take it all the way to the finish line."

~ * ~

Before school was out for the summer, I took steps to make sure Mom didn't ship me off to a wheat ranch again. I applied for a job at Jeffway grocery and they agreed to hire me when school was out. I got started the day after graduation. I learned how to stock shelves with canned goods and fix up fruits and vegetables that came in wooden boxes. I learned how to do all kinds of stupid store stuff. For a while, I even thought maybe this food business might be a good racket. People have to eat.

Grocery guys are onta-pra-newers, too!

Eventually, the owner had me drive his Model "A" Ford pickup around town, delivering groceries to those who paid a little extra. It was great fun. I had no driver's license, but the cops didn't worry much about such things. They had bigger problems to worry about, like tracking down Japanese-Americans still "at large" out there somewhere west of Highway 97.

~ * ~

That summer, the Army Air Corps announced it would spend two million dollars expanding the local airport to create a first-class airbase, to be called the Madras Army Air Base. Main Street merchants were floating on Cloud Nine. They had many meetings to talk about it, hoping and planning for this latest windfall to pump up their bottom lines, just like good-old-boy onta-pra-newers everywhere.

Men in suits began showing up—engineers, planners, architects and construction bosses—all of them looking for places to live. The local paper said that houses and sleeping rooms in private homes were needed and urged people to sign up as landlords. Ranchers went after a new crop called renters. Old homestead houses were cleaned up and put into service. Many people in town fixed up a bedroom or two and rented them out to the strangers in suits with deep pockets.

One day a stout gentleman walked up and rang our doorbell. When Mom answered, he asked if she would be willing to rent him a room. After a moment's thought, she agreed. Next thing I knew, he was huffing and puffing and dragging a huge steamer trunk upstairs. He moved into Skipper's bedroom. The lodger was Mr. Sorenson, an engineer helping design the airbase. He was a big man with a huge mound of white hair. He only stayed a few weeks and then moved back home. I think Mom got to pocket the rent money. He came and went as he pleased and didn't cause any problems for anybody.

"Why are we having this war?" I asked him once.

He looked up, surprised. "They attacked us, remember? We all have to hang together now and win this war." Then he mentioned some guy named Shakespeare and started spouting off:

> "This day is called the feast of Crispian
> He that outlives this day and comes safe home
> Will stand a tip-toe when this day is named
> And rouse him at the name of Crispian
> He that shall live this day and see old age
> Will yearly say 'Tomorrow is St. Crispian'
> Then strip his sleeves and show his scars

And say 'these wounds I had on Crispians day'
From this day to the ending of the world
But we in it shall be remembered
We few, we happy few, we band of brothers
For he today that sheds his blood with me
Shall be my brother
And gentlemen in England now a-bed
Shall think themselves accursed they were not here
And hold their manhoods cheap while any speaks
That fought with us on St. Crispian's Day"

Mr. Sorenson and his Shakespeare gave Skipper and me the creeps. It just wasn't natural somehow, especially in little old Madras. Still, he was a nice old guy and he was helping build an airbase to train bomber crews to fly over Germany and bomb some nasty Nazis like that German fighter pilot in *Mrs. Miniver*. I thought he deserved a pat on the back. With or without St. Crispian's Day, I figured he belonged with that special band of brothers who were fighting this big new war.

Most of the time, I wasn't too concerned about Mr. Sorenson. What I thought about mostly was that sonofabitch Mexican. I wasn't exactly worried about him. But he was always there in the back of my mind. Sure, I hadn't seen a trace of him since the Soap Box Derby. He seemed to have fallen off the edge of the earth. I still had those cards he gave me. They were in my sock drawer. Sometimes I took them out and looked at them and tried to make some kinda sense of it. But then I was back at Square One. What did those cards mean? What was he trying to tell me? There was no message I could make out of it, no matter how hard I tried. Okay, he gave me four cards. There was the king of spades—the last card he gave me —and the jack of spades and the queen of spades. And the first card, the ten of spades. What did they mean?

All spades. Don't spades mean something bad? I drove myself nuts trying to make some sense of it all, and then finally threw the stupid cards back in the drawer. What became of the Mexican? Did he crawl back in the hole he came out of? I sure hope so. But one thing I knew. I wasn't scared of him anymore. I knew he could've grabbed me or stabbed me a million times before and he didn't do it. I just needed to forget about him, not think about him anymore and get back to my normal life.

In September, I quit my grocery job and got ready for school. This new school year would be different. I wouldn't walk east on "B" Street to the grade school. This year I would walk five blocks south to the high school. On the first day, I took my bike. It was more dignified, somehow, more elevated and statelier to bike rather than walk. It seemed a fitting tribute to my lofty new status as a high school student, with all the honor and prestige that title bestowed.

Going into the high school that first morning, I was really glad to see all my old friends. Especially Beverly Nelson, lovely as ever and maybe ready for another necking session—if only I could just arrange another grade school graduation party. All of us walked along the wide hallways and explored the new classrooms, checked out the cafeteria and got a good feel for this new place in our lives. Though lowly freshmen, we were now members of this exclusive club called high school.

In many ways, it was a lot like grade school. I joined the freshman basketball squad, along with my former teammates, and we practiced each day getting ready for the new season. I was still in the high school band, still back in the loser row of the clarinet section. It was good to be back in school with old McKinney again. Mr. Nygaard was still our band leader. He talked me into signing up for more clarinet lessons. I plowed ahead on my metal clarinet, still trying to make sense of the stupid music and still trying to hit the right notes most of the time.

At the orientation meeting, we all got a good look at the high school principal, Mr. Edmund Kirkpatrick. He was medium height with salt-and-pepper hair and round glasses, with crooked teeth under a scraggly moustache—a Teddy Roosevelt type. He wasn't a smoothie like Mr. Baxter, but he was a nice-enough guy and seemed to have all the bases covered.

There was a new kid in our class, one who must have moved in during the summer. His name was Steve Baker. Tall and gangly, he had red hair and freckles and a goofy grin. He was a foster child and working cowboy for a cattle ranch and feedlot operation about ten miles east of town. Baker rode his horse to school each day. He never stayed after school for athletics or anything because he had to ride back home in time to finish up his ranch chores.

Each morning, he rode to school and tethered his horse to the flag pole. All day, the horse grazed happily around the school lawn until Baker rode him home that evening. He always wore the same outfit, Baker did—jeans with a big brass buckle, boots, spurs, striped shirt, and straw cowboy hat—so he looked pretty much like a real cowboy. He walked down the hallway with a bow-legged swagger, spurs jingling with each step. The teachers always made him hang up his spurs on the coat rack.

I took a liking to old Baker and we became friends. Before long, he invited me out to his place for a visit. One Saturday morning, he rode into town trailing another horse. We met in front of the courthouse. I took his other horse and swung into the saddle. We followed a gravel road running through sagebrush and bunch grass out in the middle of nowhere. We came over a little hill and he stopped.

"There it is," he said, pointing to a ranch down the road.

It was a crummy place to look at. There wasn't a tree in sight or any shade anywhere. It was an ugly cluster of weather-beaten sheds, buildings and a barn. There was a grain silo, an eighteen-wheeler truck-trailer, some bay trucks, a Cat tractor and some pickups parked here and there. On all sides were feedlots full of bawling cattle. Men on horseback rode among the cattle, sorting them out and herding them into holding pens. As we got closer, I saw men loading bales of hay onto a conveyor which carried the bales to the upper loft of the barn. Other men were loading cattle into the truck-trailer, getting ready to haul them over the mountains to Portland. I could see this place was a meat factory, pure and simple.

Baker dismounted and threw his horse's reins over a hitching rail and I did the same. We walked into the barn. Support poles gleamed along the hay-strewn walkway, polished by years of horse rubbings. The air smelled of leather, hay and manure. Horses in their stalls turned and watched us go by. One of them whinnied. Old Baker stroked its neck. He poured some oats into a feeding trough for the horse, then poured more oats into other bins among the stalls.

We walked out of the barn and across a gravel yard to the main house. The place looked more like a hideout than a home. It was a squat wooden dwelling, huddled near the ground, a low roof hanging down over the porch. The roof was old cedar shakes and the siding was built with unpainted planks and board-and-batten. We walked up the two steps and across the creaking porch and opened the front door. Inside was a big room with a long table surrounded by wooden chairs. The floor was bare planking with "south of the border" rugs scattered around. Another room had some old leather chairs, some beat-up tables with initials carved in them, a couple of reading lamps and a big round table loaded with girlie magazines. Paperback books were scattered around, along with empty beer bottles, a deck of cards, and oversize ashtrays with crushed cigarettes. In another room, wooden bunk-beds were piled high with blankets and pillows thrown back in a haphazard way.

I followed Baker into the kitchen. It had a big refrigerator, a metal sink with two sections, and a cast-iron wood stove with all kinds of pots and pans hanging overhead.

He greeted the cook, a middle-aged woman named Sally, who was cutting up potatoes for dinner. We walked back outside. Men were coming and going with a sense of great urgency. Some said hello, but nobody stopped for any chit-chat. One guy drove away in a pickup, throwing up dust in his haste to head out on some vital mission. Baker's foster father, the "Boss," was out of town on some business deal. So I didn't get to meet him. But I had to admire him. Here was a guy whose operation gave people just what they wanted—beef—and probably at top dollar prices. Here was a real authentic genuine bona fide onta-pra-newer, the same kind of onta-pra-newer I might become myself someday if I played my cards right.

We climbed on the horses and rode back into town. At the courthouse, I dismounted and gave my reins to Baker. I waved good-bye as he turned and trotted back toward the ranch with my horse in tow.

Twelve

Meanwhile, the war effort continued. Like most everybody else, Dad only had an "A" sticker for our car. He was a "non-essential" worker, so he only got four gallons of gas a week. Guys who worked in factories making war stuff—Iike Boeing in Seattle—were "essential" workers and got "B" stickers with coupons good for eight gallons a week. There was a "C" sticker for doctors and ministers and mailmen, plus an "X" card for guys in Congress and government bureaucrats and other big shots too important to walk.

The scrap-iron drive kept going, bringing in rusty old metal parts—gears and wheels and sprockets and rebar and angle iron—which piled up in growing mounds in the vacant lot behind the Chief Theater.

Some Office of Price Administration honcho told a local dairyman he couldn't raise milk prices enough to cover higher feed costs. So the dairyman quit delivering milk. After a week, the public outcry got so bad that Madras city fathers caved in and pressured the OPA into letting him raise his prices. Just like the Pied Piper handled the city fathers of Hamlin.

Construction continued on the Madras Army Air Base up on Agency Plains. They set up a rock-crusher operation east of town and built a new truck road under the high railroad bridge and up the slopes of Willow Creek canyon to the plateau. Soon big trucks pulling trailers full of crushed rock pounded the streets of Madras day and night, hauling rock uphill to the airbase construction project.

One day, some of us kids were hanging around after school in the alley behind Thomas Motors. We had ridden our bikes there for no great special reason, a group of us just talking about nothing in particular. I looked up and saw Max Kirkham coming out of the showroom, heading our way.

"Hi, Max," somebody said.

"Hi, guys," he replied. I looked at him, standing there with his head bobbing in that cocky way of his. He was a grown man, eighteen years old and just out of high school. His two little eyes were set close together and his lower jaw stuck out like a bulldog. He was dressed like an *Esquire* magazine ad—sports coat, white shirt with tie, slacks, and shined shoes. His old man had a fuel oil business and he had some phony job keeping track of the drivers. He might've even had an "X" card, for all I knew.

"Hi, lucky," somebody said.

"Wanna trade places? I had to sign up with the draft board this week."

"Oh, you'll probably get a 4-F for having the clap."

Max reared his head back and laughed. "Yeah, maybe. I've been hitting my favorite cathouse in Bend. Maybe it'll payoff."

"How much did it cost?" I asked.

"I made a deal with the madam and got two at the same time. It was different, I'll tell you that. Cost me six bucks."

"What's your favorite cathouse?"

"The Cozy Rooms. Can't beat 'em for quality and price."

The rest of us low-class morons just stood there and gaped in wonderment. Here was a guy who had the world by the tail. Here was a guy who had all the answers. I couldn't help asking him something. "Max, when do people stop screwing?"

"Never. Your daddy and mommy screw their brains out every night."

"Bullshit! "

"Bullshit, my ass! Think they stopped screwing after they had you?" I didn't have an answer. I just stood there and stared at him.

"Look, kid," he said. "You're saying your daddy and mommy don't screw their brains out every night? I'm saying they do. And they sure don't want any more kids like you. That means they gotta use rubbers."

He reached in his pocket and pulled out something that looked like three white balloons bound in an oval shape. The three-pack even had a brand name—Trojans—on the package. "Here's what they look like. Now let's try something to prove I'm right. Go home right now and check out your daddy and mommy's bedroom. There's always a little nightstand by the bed. Look in the top drawer. I'll bet you'll find some rubbers in there."

This idea was so shocking I just stood there gaping.

Suddenly he remembered he had more important business elsewhere. Without a word, he turned and strutted on down the alley to his Chevy four-door. He climbed in his car and took off.

After he was gone, I casually made some phony excuse to leave. I climbed on my bike and rode slowly toward the community hall until I was out of sight. Then I turned on the speed, made a left and rode a couple blocks, crossed the main street, made a big circle around some blocks toward Willow Creek canyon, then turned and headed home. When I got there, the place was empty. Mom had gone someplace, probably to the Jeffway store.

I sneaked into my parents' bedroom and crept up to the little nightstand sitting next to the bed. Very slowly, I slid the top drawer open and looked inside. I couldn't believe it! There in the drawer was a pack of rubbers! I picked them up and stared at them—a pack of Trojans—just like Max said! I sat there on the bed, holding the rubbers, trying to make sense of what I had discovered. It was a huge shock, like someone had hit me right in the gut!

Carefully, I put the rubbers back in the drawer just as I had found them and wandered out of the bedroom and into the living room. I plopped down on the sofa and stared out the window, trying to figure it out. Okay, so screwing wasn't just for teenagers in the back seat of cars. Screwing wasn't just for guys like Max going to a cathouse. Screwing was just an ordinary everyday function. Like eating and sleeping. I sat there on the sofa, trying to run this through my head. Okay, so everybody in town screws their brains out every night. Everybody—the teachers, the merchants, the preachers, the cops, the high school principal, all the parents—screw their brains out every night. Wow, it was just like Max said. This was a whole new way of looking at the world. And it was going to take a long time to chew it over. Maybe I would never figure it out. Did everybody screw their brains out every night? How about that Mexican bastard? Did he ever screw anybody?

~ * ~

In Madras, the war effort picked up speed. Near the end of the year, Major Lockhart landed in town. He arrived with great fanfare as commanding officer of the new airbase. He enjoyed great popularity with the locals. And he must've been popular with the Army Air Corps, too. After a few months, he was promoted to a new job as commanding officer of a brand-new airbase over in Walla Walla, Washington. He and his wife left town right after a big farewell party at the USO Club, the former Community Hall. There were speeches by some local politicians saying how they would be missed. Major Lockhart gave $300 from the Officers' Club to the local Red Cross. The men of the base gave the major and his wife a silver carving set. Then a dance started, with a sergeant from the base playing music on his accordion. There was lots of coffee and cake on the back counter by the kitchen. Local merchants, good onta-pra-newers, stood on the sidelines munching cake and thinking of all the money falling in their laps from the airbase construction and now from the Air Corps coming in to fly B-17s on bomber training missions.

~ * ~

Even with all this stuff going on, the Second World War seemed to be happening on another planet. That changed when two attacks brought the war home to Oregon. These were the first attacks by a foreign power on the continental United States since the War of 1812.

Fort Stevens, an artillery battery bunker built along the north coast during the Civil War, was a worthless concrete relic sitting there above the sand and driftwood logs in obsolete and peaceful splendor. Then, in June of 1942, it was shelled by a Japanese submarine—out of range for return fire—with seventeen rounds lobbed from its deck gun. The barrage tore up the battery's baseball diamond and scored a perfect strike on the backstop behind home plate. Three months later, a Japanese plane dropped incendiary bombs on forests along the south coast near the town of Brookings. The fires fizzled out in the rain-soaked woods.

Otherwise the war seemed real only when B-17 bombers flew over town, back from training runs in the desert. Sometimes they came in at low altitude, rattling everyone's teeth with a deafening roar. Nobody said anything about where they were going after training. No talk of bomber crews taking off from English airbases to fly real bombing missions over Germany.

Popular songs of the day brought relief from the war news and provided a sort of common warmth to the home front. This was the big-band era, with sweet and bouncy swing music. Radio shows broadcast hit songs day and night, favorites such as "In The Mood," "Don't Sit Under The Apple Tree," "Jersey Bounce" and "Juke Box Saturday Night." In the early days of the war, songs were upbeat—like "Boogie Woogie Bugle Boy of Company B"—and later wistful, like "Saturday Night Is The Loneliest Night Of The Week." Many had lyrics that told a bittersweet story, with a haunting melody.

November of 1942 brought news about the Allied invasion of North Africa at the French colony of Morocco. Americans expected the French to help and welcome them as liberators. Instead, French planes and shore batteries strafed and bombed U.S. troopships and warships. It was the Vichy French, who agreed to fight for Germany when they surrendered, so they were just living up to their contract. A deal is a deal, right? But it seemed like treachery, like some back-stabbing double cross. How could any nation betray its allies like that? Expecting a cakewalk, Americans had a full battle on their hands before landing troops ashore and finally taking the port city of Casablanca.

Here's the weird part: a movie called *Casablanca* came out about the same time as the invasion. It gave everyone a better understanding of this Vichy French deal, with the Germans calling the shots and the phony French guys keeping up appearances. There was intrigue, treachery, noble sacrifice and a love story. But the movie was more than that. It was touching and magical. Many people thought it was the best movie ever made.

When Warner Brothers produced *Casablanca,* they say, it was intended as just another Class B pot-boiler cobbled together to cash in on the war fever. Somehow it struck a chord. Everyone was struck by its conflicts, its loyalties and betrayals, its themes of love found and lost, then recovered and sacrificed to a higher cause. Good music, too. The movie features Humphrey Bogart and Ingrid Bergman, with Paul Henreid as Bergman's husband. The story is set in Rick's Café, a hotbed of refugees and smugglers and Nazis, along with those serial bad guys, Sydney Greenstreet and Peter Lorre. When Claude Rains, the crooked chief of police, orders his cops to "round up the usual suspects," it means Bogart is off the hook for shooting the German major just before giving his letter of transit to Bergman and Henreid so they can catch the plane to Portugal and freedom.

Earlier, Bergman walks into Rick's Café, and heads for Sam at the piano. She asks Sam to play a song recalling a love affair with Bogart in Paris. He claims he can't remember the tune. Bergman says she'll hum it for him. Sam starts to play. He remembers it after all.

Bogart, hearing this, rushes up and yells at Sam, "I told you never to play that song again!" Sam nods in the direction of Bergman. Rick is shocked to see her again. Later he sits with a bottle of booze and moans, "Of all the gin joints in all the world, why did she have to pick mine?" This movie served hogwash of the highest order, set in a never-never land of high stakes, big emotions and unforgettable acting. When it played at the Chief Theater, the little family from Willow Creek sat with their heads together in a kind of divine rapture, offering no criticism or comments. Certainly none of the older brother yelling "Mush!" and stomping out. This was the ultimate Academy Awards judgment and *Casablanca* won hands-down.

~ * ~

Back at Madras High School, the days went by without too many problems. We studied algebra, English literature, history, economics and other stuff that probably did us no harm and maybe even a little good.

Even though a freshman, I had been playing clarinet in the high school band for over a year. But I was real bad at it. A girl, Debbie Olson, was First Clarinet. She was good and she knew it. She sat two rows ahead of me, the loser sitting back in the loser section. From my seat, I could see her blonde pony-tail and chubby arms and her puffed-out cheeks blowing on that black horn like crazy.

I hated being in the back row of the clarinet section. I hated being a loser. But if I challenged somebody ahead of me, I always got beat. At least I knew better than to challenge old Debbie. She would've whipped my butt. Boy, was she good! Boy, was she proud! She had always been high-and-mighty about her exalted status and ignored me like I didn't exist.

But she surprised me one day after band practice. She actually came up and said hello. "You're hitting the notes better," she said, looking at me through those rimless glasses of hers. "How much do you practice these days?"

"Oh, maybe a couple hours a week."

"That's not enough. You need more practice. Why don't you come over to my house right after school? Bring your clarinet and we'll practice together. Come in the back door."

"Okay. You still live by the grade school? The yellow house?"

She nodded. "I have to go home early and vacuum the place. I'll be finished before you get there. See you after school."

Then she went back to her seat up front. She packed up her clarinet, black and beautiful like Benny Goodman's. I packed up my old metal job, the kind you never see in the movies.

Soon as gym was over, 1 grabbed my clarinet case, jumped on my bike and took off for Debbie's house. Why did she want to practice with me? Maybe she could teach me some new tricks.

From the high school, 1 coasted down the street heading for downtown. 1 sailed past the Chief Theater and hung a right at the bank. I followed "B" Street several blocks, turned left and went down the street where 1 could see her house. It was a big two-story yellow house on the corner. I turned right, then took a left turn down an alley to a board fence behind her house. I pushed the gate open, walked my bike inside the yard and leaned it up against the garage. Then I grabbed my clarinet case, opened the back door and went inside. I went in through the kitchen and looked around but didn't see anybody. So I wandered into the dining room and living room. I saw her case on the piano, so 1 set my case next to it.

"Debbie! Where are you?"

"Upstairs! Come on up!"

I walked up the stairs, bewildered. How could we practice on the second floor with no instruments?

"I'm in here," came her voice through a door. "It's my bedroom. Come on in."

I opened the door and walked in. The shades were closed and it was dark, but I could see a candle burning over in the corner. I saw a collection of stuffed animal toys looking down from rows of shelves on all sides, piles of them. There were a panda bear, a lion, a raccoon, a tiger, a big stuffed rabbit, a frog, a goat, a fox, a monkey, a bear, and a pig, all of them staring at me in the flickering candlelight. Then I heard a phonograph start playing. I recognized the song. It was "Dancing in the Dark" with Artie Shaw playing his clarinet.

Suddenly Debbie appeared. She was wearing an Hawaiian grass skirt and fuzzy red halter with exposed arms and open midriff. Wow! Without her glasses, she looked exotic—especially with black make-up under her eyes like Cleopatra—and smelling of perfume. It was a heavy dose, like she had jumped in a barrel of the stuff. She twirled around, with no underpants, and I could see her snatch. Wow! What was this all about?

Five Cards and a Cathouse

"Take off your shoes and socks," she said. What for? Was she gonna teach me some kind of Hawaiian dance? I did as I was told. Then she came up real close and leaned into me.

"Take off my halter," she said. With trembling fingers, I got hold of two buttons along the bottom and unbuttoned them. Then she turned her back to me. Still shaking, I untied a strap that went around her neck. In a flash, she pulled off the garment and flung it across the room. Then she turned to face me once again. Wow! I gaped at her grapefruit-size knockers staring back at me, nipples sticking out like pencil erasers. I stood there, spellbound, fumbling with my own pullover sweater. She grabbed it at the bottom and I put my arms straight up—as if surrendering— as she pulled the sweater off, unbuttoned my shirt and threw both away. I took off my undershirt as she yanked out my belt, unzipped my fly and pulled down my pants. In the full spirit of things now, I kicked my pants away with a vengeance. Then she pulled down my shorts. I stood there like a zombie, my little dick at full attention. Then she dropped to her knees and took my dick in her mouth. Holy shit—the big boys never told me about this! I stood there, watching, as she worked it with her mouth and tongue and lips. My God, I thought, no wonder she's such a good clarinet player! I was getting all fired up when she stopped. I stood there, not knowing what to do, wondering what was next. She put her hands on my chest and shoved and I fell over backwards onto her bed. Then she pulled off her skirt and jumped on top of me.

We went round and round, like rag dolls in a washing machine, a storm of twisting and turning bodies, a tornado of groping, grasping and grunting, a whirlpool of penetration and ejaculation, all with dozens of stuffed animals staring down in disbelief.

Then it was over. Debbie pushed me off and jumped up and ran over to a table in the corner. She blew out the candle. She stopped the music. Then she grabbed a bottle of Coke, popped the top, shook it and shoved it up her snatch as the fizz exploded inside of her.

I watched all this with fascination. Somehow, I knew Debbie had been down this road before. I laid back on the bed, tired in a good way, just wanting to sleep a loongggg time—

SPLAT! She dumped the rest of the Coke on my face!

"What the hell was that for?"

"My mother gets off work in ten minutes! You gotta get out of here! Now!"

I crawled off the bed, found my shorts and jammed them on. I found my belt, pulled on my pants and buttoned up my shirt. I put on my socks and my shoes, but couldn't get them laced up fast enough.

"Come on!" she yelled. "You gotta go! Now!"

"Okay! Okay! I'm going fast as I can!"

It wasn't fast enough. Debbie grabbed my sweater and pulled it down over my head so hard it hurt my ears.

"Come on!" she yelled, as I tried to lace up my shoes. She pulled me to my feet and pushed me out of her bedroom. Somehow, I stumbled down the stairs. At the piano, I grabbed my clarinet case just before she shoved me on through the living room and dining room. She pushed me through the kitchen and out the back door as I was still trying to zip up my pants.

"Get outta here!" she yelled again, slamming the back door.

I threw my clarinet case in the basket and rode my bike down the alley to the next street. I stopped and got off the bike to lace up my shoes and zip up my pants. Then I thought about what had happened. Okay, I got out of there before her mother showed up. That was good. To size up what happened—Wow!!—so *that's* what all the guys were talking about! So *that's* what the East Lake Girl meant when she wanted to "fool around!" Now I knew what all the excitement was all about. It wasn't too bad. Oh, sure, I would've preferred a different ending. Maybe a little more affection at the end. Maybe a lot less panic about her mother coming home. But so what? This sex stuff seemed to be worth all the build-up. Anyway, I had passed a major milestone in my life. And it didn't really matter anymore if I was still the lousiest clarinet player in the whole high school band.

~ * ~

In March, Dad got new "Orders from Salem" transferring him over to Pendleton to supervise some new highway construction. Skipper and I were excited about moving over to this big city of ten thousand people. We knew they had a big-time rodeo called the Pendleton Round-Up. Dad said they also had a night-time pageant called Happy Canyon running during the whole Round-Up week. Sounded like lots of fun.

School life in Madras continued. An unofficial holiday of the year was April Fool's Day on the first day of April. It was considered very important to play a practical joke on somebody. Everybody loved having this excuse to pull some pranks. There were a couple of classics that nailed the suckers each year. An older high school guy, for example, would use a Zippo lighter to heat up a stupid nickel and drop it in the hallway. Then some sap always came along, grabbed it and got his fingers burned. "April Fool!" the older guy yelled, jumping out from behind a door as the sucker stood there soaking his fingers in his mouth.

Another favorite scam required a wallet and about fifty feet of invisible fishing line. A wallet just lying there on the sidewalk or on a path through a vacant lot is hard to resist. Soon as some idiot bent over to pick it up, the wallet would suddenly scoot away. The sap always lunged for it, like a fish after a fly, before some grinning lout jumped out from behind a fence yelling "April Fool! April Fool!"

It was getting on toward the end of March when Steve Baker talked to me about riding out to his ranch again the following Saturday. Without even thinking about April Fool's Day, I said okay. He said to meet him in front of the Jeffway store at ten o'clock.

When Saturday came around, I walked over to the main drag and sauntered down the board sidewalk past the false-front stores to Jeffway Grocery. When I got to the store, old Baker was standing there with a sack of groceries. He was standing between two saddled horses, each one tethered to a brass ring embedded in the board planks of the sidewalk.

"Here's yours," he said, as he untied the reins of one horse and handed them to me. I took the reins, put a foot in the stirrup and swung aboard. It was a quarter horse, of course, beautiful chestnut color. Baker said it was a gelding "the Boss" had won in a poker game in Reno. Then he lifted up the sack of groceries.

"Help me carry this out to the ranch," he said. I reached down and took the sack. The paper made a slight crackling sound. Suddenly my horse jumped up and came down—BAM!—and I bounced high off the saddle. I dropped the sack and grabbed the horn with both hands as the horse took off running and bucking down the street. The ground went racing by, then fell away and came rushing back—WHAM! —as I bounced high off the saddle again. The horse kept running and bucking and turned down a side street. I grabbed the horn tighter, desperately trying to glue myself to the saddle. The horse jumped again and came down—BAM!—as—I bounced high off the saddle. He raced down the street and bucked again— —WHAM!—and again—BAM!—as I bounced again and again off the saddle.

Then the horse stopped. He just stood there, still as a statue. I looked around. We were behind the Chief Theater, right in the middle of the scrap-iron collection. Right between piles of scrap iron. Heaps of rusty gears, sprockets, wheels, rebar and shards of angle iron sticking up like spears.

Old Baker came riding up, slapping his legs and laughing like a maniac. "April Fool!!" he yelled, laughing so hard he could barely say the words. "April Fool! That horse spooks at the sound of paper! Don't worry, he'll be okay now!"

I jumped off the horse. "Baker, you son-of-a-bitch! Take this goddamn horse and shove it up your ass!"

His jaw dropped in astonishment; his face stricken. He shook his head, shocked that anyone could misunderstand his harmless little cowboy joke. Then he leaned over and took the horse's reins. He turned his horse around and trotted back toward the ranch, trailing the maverick horse. I walked home and tried to forget all about this crappy April Fool's Day.

~ * ~

Before we knew it, the school year was over and so was our time in Madras. A few days before the moving van was set to arrive, we got some cardboard boxes and started packing up. By then, Skipper and I knew the routine all too well. We stuffed the boxes full of shirts, underwear, pants and everything else in our bedrooms. We helped fill other boxes full of all kinds of stuff from the bathroom, living room, kitchen and garage until everything was packed up and ready to go.

Then the moving van showed up. Once again, two guys got out and went to work with hand-trucks loading all the big stuff. They packed in our bicycles and all the little boxes into the spaces between the big stuff. Then they closed the van doors and took off.

Everybody climbed in the Plymouth, ready to go. Everybody but me. I was in the house getting a last drink of water from the kitchen faucet, kinda taking my time. Truth is, I hated to leave this old house and this tiny cow town. I'd had a lot of fun living here and some great adventures with good friends like Todd McKinney.

And how could I forget that magical night here at my eighth-grade graduation party when I got into that kissing match with the beautiful Beverly Nelson? I wandered outside in a dreamy state suddenly shattered by the sound of Mom telling me to hurry up.

I got in the car and we took off for Pendleton. We drove north for about an hour, while I went into a trance of memories—

~ * ~

I open my eyes and look around. Our old Plymouth is rolling along Highway 30 with the engine putting out a contented motor sound. Old Veronica, on the other side of the back seat, is looking out her window in a kind of hypnotic trance. Maybe she is thinking of the friends she had left behind. Skipper is sound asleep, leaning into her for support, or maybe some sisterly comfort. I can see we're heading east with the broad Columbia River on our left and barren hills on the right. It's pretty blah and boring country, if you want to know the truth.

This is uncharted territory for me and it seems like it just keeps going on forever. We follow the Columbia along its south bank, the highway winding through rocks and bunchgrass below barren cliffs of black lava. We slow down and come into a village called Arlington, an oasis of cottonwood trees and houses, and keep heading east on Highway 30.

Dad and Mom sit in the front, staring in silence at the road ahead. Skipper wakes up and looks around. He's got a half-assed look on his face, like he's forgotten what is going on. Maybe he's wondering about this new town and whether he could find any friends there. Veronica was still looking out the window, maybe wondering about her boyfriend, Bill Whitmore. He is in the Air Corps pilot training back in Kansas or some place.

As we roll along, Dad suddenly pipes up. "We'll leave the Columbia River at Boardman. But if we followed the river up into Washington, we'd soon come to Hanford. That's where they're working on that new secret weapon."

"What secret weapon?"

"Nobody knows what it's all about. Some kind of new secret weapon is all I've heard."

"Maybe it's some kind of poison gas."

"Naw. We've got enough poison gas already. Anyway, we can't use poison gas. It's against the rules."

"They have rules in war?"

"Sure. You can't shoot prisoners. And you can't use poison gas. They learned that lesson in the last war."

"Maybe they'll outlaw this new secret weapon."

"No, they always give you one war to try out something new. The next war, yeah, maybe they'll outlaw it then."

We drove into Boardman; it only had a few houses and a couple gas stations. Dad pulls into a station and stops by a pump. An old guy comes right out of his little shack and pops our hood. He checks the oil and fiddles with the belts and checks the water. Then he gets down on his knees and checks all four tires for air pressure. Only then does he come around and look at Dad.

"Fill 'er up," says Dad. "Don't worry, I got enough coupons."

The old guy nods and grabs the gas hose. While he's filling 'er up, we all get out and head for the bathrooms. When we come back, Dad gets all his "A" coupons out and is digging in his wallet for cash to pay the guy. We climb in, Dad fires up the Plymouth and away we go.

We come to a junction and take the road to the right. I can see we're leaving the river and heading out across a sagebrush desert.

"This road is a tangent all the way to Pendleton," says Dad.

There he goes with that engineer talk again. "What do you mean, tangent?"

"This highway is a tangent. It goes in a straight line almost all the way to Pendleton."

"Why don't you just say straight line?"

No answer. Maybe he's thinking about it, wondering why he doesn't use plain English like everybody else.

We pass a weird landscape of black cement mounds, just sitting out there in the middle of nowhere. "That's the Umatilla Ordnance Depot," says Dad. "It's where the Army stores bombs and shells and all kinds of stuff. They even have some of that poison gas we were talking about."

Sounds like we're in a real war zone. What a crazy place Oregon is right now...Jap submarines along the coast, shelling Fort Stevens and bombing the woods outside Brookings. Across the river, in Washington, they're nailing together some kind of secret weapon. And right here on Highway 30, the Army has all these black bunkers full of shells and bombs. And poison gas.

In case they need to use it, rules or no rules. All this stuff going on all over the world. Evelyn's husband Chuck Foster in the Army back in Mississippi.

Veronica's boyfriend Bill Whitmore back in Kansas was learning how to fly bombers for the Air Corps. All the older guys have gone to war. And here I am, not yet old enough to fight. Not much to care about or worry about. Except that Mexican bastard. Why isn't *he* in the Army? Must be a wetback, an illegal. What does he want from me, anyway? I'm not scared of him anymore. Not scared that he's going to stab me or anything. He could've done that a million times already. Maybe he wants to kidnap me. No, Dad doesn't have enough money for any big ransom payoff. Will he find me in Pendleton? Sure as hell he will. No doubt about it. He's got some kind of inside track on me. I know damn well that sonofabitch will find me again. No doubt about it.

We drive through more sagebrush, once crossing some green bottomlands with a creek running through. We keep rolling and come into wheat country, drive past a grain elevator, and keep cruising along. Then we follow the highway around a curve and get our first look at Pendleton. Dad pulls off and parks on a shoulder of gravel.

Below, in the wide valley of the Umatilla River, lies a soft green sea of cottonwood trees sheltering a town of ten thousand people. It's a huge city. It's a whole new world—shady and civilized—a place of hotels and hospitals, of woolen mills and canneries and lumber mills, of green parks and playgrounds, a main drag with four blocks of two-story stone buildings selling everything from bourbon and bacon to saddles, steaks and salt licks.

We follow Highway 30 into town, past the Roundup grounds with a big park and through a residential section and into the business section. We continue on past blocks of commercial buildings and into the east-side residential district. Dad seems to know where he's going. He takes a left off Court Avenue, works his way over to SE 12th Street, and pulls up in front of our new home.

Skipper and I jump out to explore the place, running clear around the house. Dad and Mom get out, followed by Veronica. They open the front door and we all file inside and look around. It's a good-sized, four-bedroom house with a big living room.

"Not too bad," I say.

"It's owned by the Highway Department," says Dad.

That makes sense, the backyard goes right up to the cyclone fence around the paved yard with the gravel piles and equipment sheds and Dad's office.

Not long after that, the moving van shows up. They pull around and back up to the front steps. The guys lay a bridge from the truck to the floor. Then they haul in the refrigerator, piano, stuffed chairs, sofa, tables, floor radio, bed frames, and mattresses. After that, they carry in our bicycles and all the boxes full of little stuff. Pretty much the same old routine we've gone through so many times before.

The first chore is to get the bed frames set up in each bedroom, plus box springs, mattresses and bedding—for a place to sleep that night—then we quit all the moving-in work. That can wait. We all climb back in the car for a tour of our new hometown.

Dad drives us down Byers Avenue and we come out on Main Street. He hangs a left and we slowly cruise along the Main drag. Very impressive. There's a lineup of two-story stone buildings anchored by six-story hotels at each end. There are several restaurants, along with bars, taverns and two movie theaters. There's a drug store, department store, a couple of banks, music store, five-and-dime, grocery store, furniture store, bakery, hardware store, saddle shop, clothing store, newspaper office, plus lots of upstairs offices with lawyers, dentists, doctors, insurance guys certified public accountants—just about every onta-pra-newer you could ever hope to find in a single place.

We drive south along the main street, across the Union Pacific tracks, and up a hill to another residential area surrounding the high school and football field. Then we turn around and come back down off the hill on the same street and cruise the main drag in the opposite direction. We cross a bridge over the Umatilla River and drive through some real swanky neighborhoods clear out to the golf club. Then we turn around and retrace our route.

Dad parks the car and we walk along the downtown sidewalks. The place is swarming with Air Corps enlisted men saluting officers they meet along the street. Guess they have an airbase here, too. Lots of people crowd the sidewalks heading for a bar or movie. Dad finds a restaurant he likes, so we all follow him inside for a big dinner. Then we get in the car and head back to our new home in Pendleton.

For the next couple days, we work our little butts off getting all our stuff unpacked from the boxes and crammed into different places. We get all the kitchen stuff put in the cupboards and shelves under the counters. We get our bedrooms filled up with our clothes. We put all the tools and stuff out in the garage, along with our bikes, and hook up the floor radio.

The refrigerator is hooked up and working. The dining room table is in the dining room with all the chairs around it. Looks like we've done everything.

As we finish up all this moving-in, I get kinda restless and want to get out of there. Just for a change of scenery, you might say. I go back to the garage and get my bicycle out. Skipper wants to grab his bike and come along. But somehow, I don't want him along this time. I want to explore this place on my own, to think my own thoughts, without anyone else around or anything else grabbing my attention.

I jump on my bike and head in a southerly direction and come to what they call a viaduct—Highway 30 coming down off the hill on concrete columns—so you can cross underneath and avoid the traffic. I ride down Emigrant Avenue and stop to explore Til Taylor Park. It has a horseback statue of the legendary lawman killed during a jailbreak back in the day.

I follow Emigrant west, past the courthouse and a church, and finally arrive at the Temple Hotel. I park my bike in a little stand just outside the main doorway.

A train whistle suddenly shatters the low murmur of car traffic. A train is coming in. I walk a block to the station. Soon a big steam locomotive rumbles by in a slow and stately manner, its drivers and wheels pretending to work but just coasting along, bells ringing and steam hissing from a thousand vents. The coal car comes along next, followed by a string of passenger cars. They're full of GIs—soldiers—most of them smiling and waving at those of us watching.

The train stops with a series of bangs as each car runs into its friend in front. There's a silence, a kind of expectation that things are about to happen. Sure enough, some ladies wheel up a metal cart with coffee-making equipment and piles of doughnuts and dozens of plastic cups. They make the coffee and pour coffee into cups and hand them out, along with doughnuts, to the GIs who are leaning out the windows to receive this welcome offering.

As I stand there watching this, I feel a hand on my shoulder. I turn around—it's the Mexican! I'm shocked to see him again. But not scared. Not anymore. I know he could've stabbed me a million times or grabbed me if he wanted to. I was just plain pissed-off, if you want to know the truth.

"What are you doing here?" I yell. "Why in hell do you keep following me?"

He looks at me with a slight little smile.

"Take it easy, kid."

"Take it easy! Take it easy! With you following me everywhere?"

"Yeah, take it easy. Look, I got somethin' for ya. This is your last card."

I grab it out of his hand. It's the ace of spades.

"What's this bullshit all about, anyway?"

"Follow me and you'll find out."

He turns and walks away, back toward the downtown district. I'm curious now, curious enough to follow and then catch up and walk alongside him. We walk back to Emigrant, cross Main Street and end up back at the Temple Hotel. To my surprise, he leads me around behind the hotel and into an alley. I'm not scared, for some reason, and not even pissed-off at him anymore. We walk along the alley, past some big garbage cans and beat-up cars and come to an old wooden garage. He gestures toward a narrow wooden staircase hidden just behind the garage. He starts climbing the steps. I stop for a second, some touch of fear coming over me. But he looks back and smiles with a look that seems almost friendly. Still curious, I take the first step and another step and another step and then another. We come to the top of the garage and step onto a planked catwalk over the flat roof of another building and climb up more steps to a landing in front of a steel door.

He raps on the door twice and I can hear the lock move. The door opens to the inside. Behind it stands a beautiful girl, a brunette about twenty, dressed in white shorts and halter top, smiling at the Mexican.

"Hi, Manny," she says, giving him a pat on the shoulder.

"Hi, Angie," he replies, tapping her butt as she giggles and skips down the hallway. In the distance, I can see two other girls in similar outfits, talking and laughing like they don't have a care in the world.

The Mexican goes to a door and gently knocks. "Yes, come in," says a soft female voice. He opens it and I follow him inside. We enter a large room with black furniture on a thick white carpet and red velour walls with oil paintings in white frames, and some potted palms scattered around.

In the center sits a lady in a light blue formal kind of beaded gown. She has a quiet dignity affirming well-bred elegance, with a smooth face and dazzling white smile. Her hair has a soft silver luster, combed and gathered into beautiful tresses. Her black eyes shine with a look of love and compassion.

"Hello, Manuel," she says. "Please bring Hamilton over here and sit down."

"How come you know my name?"

She gives the Mexican a little smile.

"I've known about you all your life. Manuel here has kept me well informed about you."

What? She's known about me all my life? Why does she care that much about me? Who is she? What's going on here? And there's something else I'm curious about.

"Is this a cathouse? A whorehouse?"

She winced. "Oh please, Hamilton, let's not be vulgar. I'm running a business here. I give people what they want. That's the secret of business, you know. I get merchants, mill workers, lawyers and doctors. I get cowboys and Indians—especially during the Round-Up—and I even get the mayor and police chief. They come in the back way like you did. It's a business, a good business, and I'm very good at it."

"Okay. So how come you know so much about me?"

She pauses and looks up at the ceiling. "I don't know how to put this tactfully, so I'll just come out with it. I'm your aunt, Hamilton. I'm your Aunt Karla, your mother's half-sister. I'll bet she never told you about me, did she?"

My Aunt Karla? Holy crap! I looked at her through a kind of fog, not knowing what to think.

"She never told you, did she?"

I shake my head.

"That's okay. I was always the black sheep of the family. They wrote me off years ago. For some reason, though, I want to have some part of the family. That part is you, Hamilton. I want you to be my family. We would keep it quiet, of course. It would be our little secret, just you and me. I won't bother you at all. I just ask that you call me now and then. Maybe come by and see me from time to time."

"Yeah, I could do that, I guess. Wait a minute! What was all that with the cards?"

She laughs suddenly, a hearty laugh full of love.

"Oh, that was my little joke. A symbolic gesture, you might say."

"But those cards scared the hell out of me! They were all spades! Spades mean doomsday! The end! Spades mean curtains!"

She laughs again, enjoying the moment, I guess.

"Manuel gave you five cards, right? Do you remember what they were?"

"Sure. First, he gave me a ten of spades. Then a jack of spades. Then a queen of spades—" She's laughing like a little girl now, thoroughly delighted.

"Then a king of spades," she giggles.

"Then an ace of spades. Right?"

"That's right! Scared the crap out of me!"

"I'm sorry we frightened you, Hamilton. That was my little joke. Don't you understand what those cards mean?"

"Hell no, I don't!"

"What you're holding, with those cards, is a royal flush. It's the best hand in poker. With a royal flush, you pick up the whole pot on the table."

"But I'm not in a poker game."

"Yes, you are. And so is everyone else."

"Something else bothers me. We moved a lot. How did Manuel find me each time?"

"His best friend runs the janitor service for the highway office in Salem. He read your father's personnel file every week."

"So Manuel knows exactly where we live?"

"Yes, always. We are so thrilled to hear about your father being transferred to Pendleton. I think we knew about it before he did." She giggled slightly in that soft lovely way again.

"Wow! And I always thought I could get away from him—"

"Okay, Hamilton, time to get serious. Here's the deal. You become my unofficial family. I give you twenty percent of the business.

I'll have my law firm set up a trust fund. You take possession when you come of age. In the meantime, your profits are building up every day."

"Wow! Will this make me an onta-pra-newer?"

"Yes, dear Hamilton. This makes you an onta-pra-newer."

Awesome! I can't believe it!! It's like that movie where Humphrey Bogart says, "I think this is the beginning of a beautiful friendship."

Meet Ken Hodge

Ken Hodge spent his boyhood years in central Oregon during the thirties and forties. The Great Depression somehow missed this region of snow-capped mountains overlooking small towns recently carved from irrigated sagebrush desert. Carefree days for kids. No television or video games, but something better—friends and freedom and the whole outdoors to find adventure.

Holding a BBA degree from the University of Oregon, Hodge followed a career in public relations and community development. Now retired, he has written a light-hearted YA novel marinated in the history of those times, inspired by his own experiences and his off-the-wall sense of humor.

Letter to Our Readers

Enjoy this book?

You can make a difference.

As an independent publisher, Wings ePress, Inc. does not have the financial clout of the large New York publishers. We can't afford large magazine spreads or subway posters to tell people about our quality books.

But we do have something much more effective and powerful than ads. We have a large base of loyal readers.

Honest reviews help bring the attention of new readers to our books.

If you enjoyed this book, we would appreciate it if you would spend a few minutes posting a review on the site where you purchased this book or on the Wings ePress, Inc. webpages at: https://wingsepress.com/

Thank You

Visit Our Website

For The Full Inventory
Of Quality Books:

Wings ePress.Inc
https://wingsepress.com/

Quality trade paperbacks and downloads
in multiple formats,
in genres ranging from light romantic comedy
to general fiction and horror.
Wings has something for every reader's taste.
Visit the website, then bookmark it.
We add new titles each month!

Wings ePress Inc.
3000 N. Rock Road
Newton, KS 67114

www.ingramcontent.com/pod-product-compliance
Lightning Source LLC
LaVergne TN
LVHW011828060526
838200LV00053B/3942